"FEELING FREE"

Emotional Redemption in Christ

By

A. Philip Parham

(All Rights Reserved)

Author of *Letting God: Christian Meditations for Recovery*
(Harper San Francisco, 1987, revised 2001)

Acknowledgements

—ᙡᙡ—

I am indebted to so many persons. To J. Keith Miller, I give thanks for his guidance and healing friendship. To Ron and Doris Thomson, friends of encouragement and joy, I give my constant love. For friends of deliverance, Jack and Burdine Johnson, Bill and M.F. Johnson plus Neil and Pat Hector, I am so grateful. To Betsy Tice White, editor, who is not only a whiz at editing but also my wise woman in the faith, I bow the knee. I salute Doug Dodge, who taught me so much while I attended his lectures and workshops, especially at the Meadows, and so clearly interpreted Pia Mellody's theories on abuse. To my colleague and former boss, Herman Green, *gracias amigo*, for your valued support and trust. I am obliged to Wayne Fehr's rich and insightful lectures at a clergy retreat at Cloudcroft, New Mexico, along with his helpful book, "Spiritual Wholeness for Clergy." My gratitude goes also to Richard White and William O'Hanlon, who helped teach me narrative solution-focused therapy at several stellar workshops.

To John DeFoore for his teachings on hope and responsibility and his use of hula hoops. To Dr. Tracy Gordy and Dr. Dan Blunk, God bless you, for your spiritual and professional friendship and curative words. Above all others, I thank my life partner of over 50 years, Ruth Parham, for loving, honoring and cherishing me and our family

Table of Contents

Preface: Nature and Nativity ix
Introduction: Core Feelings xix

  1. From Anger to Courage 29
  2. From Fear to Wisdom 49
  3. From Pain to Sensitivity.................................69
  4. From Shame to Spirituality...........................87
  5. From Abuse to Friendship...........................109
  6. From Vulnerability to Respect 131
  7. From Selfishness to Serenity.........................149
  8. From Grief to Gratitude 169
  9. From Surprise to Surrender..........................189
10. From Loneliness to Love 209
11. From Desire to Fulfillment...........................229

PREFACE

—⚍—

Life has lessons. In my lifetime, experience has not been the best teacher but the only one. Some have been personal, even private experiences; most have been pastoral and professional. As I have attempted to offer a positive and hopeful ministry to parishioners and counselees, what has struck me and stuck to me the most has been my inescapable trust in the natural and in nature. Embracing and appreciating the natural world has almost automatically led me to expect and look for a supernatural world. It is a marvel to me how the divine seems woven into and inherent in all existence.

From childhood, I have been somehow led through my own human existence and consciousness to look with wonder within. Going on from there, it has seemed only natural to look beyond myself for more of the same in others and in the world around me. For me, this awareness has been usual, anticipated and normative. Experience of the mystical and mysterious, asleep and awake, infuses my life with excitement. Such mystic moments come to me for the most part with people, while others come within the larger world of nature. I find so much of life right here at ground level - wondrous, beautiful, and tremendous, without even looking into the heavens. The metaphysical has always appeared to me in the physical realm. "It's only natural," I often say, for that is how I have experienced what is often called spiritual and divine.

Whenever Jesus used nature stories involving soil, seeds, wind, rain, storms, fishing, friends, brothers and sisters, mothers and fathers, coins, sheep, doors, water, bread, wine, weddings, faith, life, death and new life, he made it all seem so perfectly natural and real. As he used such down-to-earth examples to deepen our understanding of God by his own, he was speaking my language and still does. Most of my spiritual insights have been of this world and not out of it. I am sure my psychiatrist friends will be glad to hear that!

Professional insights into human personality, character, temperament and disposition have come about for me, other than through my training and God's grace, what we usually call common sense. Perceptions, needs, wants and feelings seem to reside in every one of us. Having initially sensed this wonder within myself, I later came to enlarge that wonder at the marvel of life so that it extends to all animate beings and nature.

What's New?

One particular theme that weaves itself into my clinical experience is nativity - newness, birth, renewal and rebirth. The word "native," meaning natural-born, shares its word-root with "nativity." What is native to us may come to be understood as a nativity, even as an epiphany – a manifestation of the essential meaning of something, often coming suddenly, or as an appearance of the divine. We often speak of "native sons and daughters" as well as "native intelligence" and refer to the aboriginal population of this continent as Native Americans. When we speak of our "native land," the nation we are born into, we seem to mean that such belonging is natural – our God-given starting place in life. At other times, however, we may glamorize the "noble savage" as an innocent and naïve native, whose so-called primitive ways are automatically good and beneficent.

Yet, on reflection we all know better. Obviously, acting in whatever way comes naturally is not always healthy and helpful. William Golding's children, who went brutally native in his book *Lord of the Flies* is one such portrayal of this truth. We have many natural urges that can be destructive. This fact was brilliantly described by Deborah Mathis in her column of September 28th, 2001 in the El Paso Times: "Not every natural reaction is meant to be entertained. Civilization, after all is a constant struggle against the id. It requires many natural instincts to be corralled, calibrated, or deferred. If we give into every innate feeling, we may as well be crocodiles."

Nevertheless, I sincerely believe that God expects us to be more natural than unnatural, and more naturally human than inhuman or inhumane.

Part of our overall health lies in making contact with the constructive natural inclinations within us – the "good" –while resisting the destructive natural inclinations – the "evil." In the Episcopal Book of Common Prayer in Holy Baptism this resistance is incorporated into our baptismal vows when we are asked to "renounce the evil powers of this world which corrupt and destroy the creatures of God?" Such evil is indeed powerful and lies within as well as rages without.

For more than twenty-five years, I practiced the art of pastoral psychotherapy and shared over a thousand sessions annually with very special persons. To me it was, truly, practice. I prayed often that I would practice long enough and well enough so that some day I got it somewhat right. I also prayed that the counselees and I were on a healing path together in each session, leading eventually to what would become good or at least better. Ideally, we would enter holy ground together and find God's benediction.

During these special times, there were only a few meetings in which I failed to ask, "What now?" "What's next?" and "What's new?" All three questions generally elicited responses that connected in a practical way with the present and future. I seldom raised these questions, however, without harking back to information we had earlier uncovered from the person's past – moving from *un*covery into *dis*covery and *re*covery.

Remembering

God often surprises us with a unique version of grace and justice that is extremely realistic and calls us into remembering or to "Re Membering." We are welcomed into reconnection, where our broken parts are repaired and put back together. Our members (membranes) are re-joined and re-membered. Orthopedic surgeons often do this operation of sewing up, even providing complete new replacements for our members - our arms, legs, joints and ligaments. Salvation is such a process of pieces coming together, where persons are stitched back together. The Great Physician, by means of spiritual orthopedic operations, makes our souls and spirits whole, healthy and workable again.

Religion and Spirituality

Religion and remember are similar words with almost identical meanings. Re Ligion or re-ligio is much like re-membering. Ligament comes from ligio. To be re (again) ligamented (connected) is what religion does. Our religious forms, rituals, ceremonies and structures put together, reconnect, and tie together our spiritual substance and values.

Spirituality is the substance. Religion is the form. Spirituality or faith is the inward and religion is the outward and visible. Spirituality vitalizes; religion shapes. Spirituality is the horse; religion is the carriage. We know that our spiritual vitality is essential and necessary to recovery and life, whereas religion is helpful and nice. Religion is the package not the content, the wrapping not the present inside. I rejoice in my packaging as an Episcopalian, but I could exist without it. Nevertheless, I would have to follow another denomination's wrapping in order to stay within the Christian faith.

Our religious wraps are a great comfort here in this life, but of no use in the life to come. Some of us have no use for religion now, but I have not found suitable substitutes for the tried and true faith handed down by the saints. Jesus found his religion vital and useful in his life. Who can do better?

Recovery

Recovery is another word like remember and religion. The core word is "cover" or covering. When we admit our powerlessness, when we come to believe, when we make a conscious decision to turn our wills over to God, we are running for cover. We are seeking safety in our surrender into the sheltering arms of divinity. Our shield and security is a gracious God who beckons to us to be re-covered, to be covered again, blanketed and tucked in, hidden and protected by love and hope. We can always run to God for cover, with Christ - our covering.

Recovery is such a sweet sounding word and reality. What an inviting process recovery is, leading us to *un-cover* (the old, the tried and true as well as the bad and bitter) to *dis-cover* (the new, fresh and renewed as well as the difficult and demanding) so can truly begin our life-long pilgrimage of *re-covery,* (embraced and enfolded by a life full of "priceless gifts of serenity)."

The greatest satisfaction of therapy is not just uncovering the past and doing personal archaeology, but having the thrill of discovery and the on-going experience of recovery, especially the freshness of looking ahead and moving forward. That is where the importance of nativity comes in.

Newborns

Newness is hope beckoning us into tomorrow. Nativity is birth, happening any time, anywhere. Although a natural event, birthing usually hurts and in the King James Version of the Bible, Jesus called it travail and anguish. (John 16:21) Yet, he focused on the joy that follows delivery, which becomes oblivious to the previous labor pain. Such birth and deliverance leaves me in awe, not only witnessing newborn babies in delivery rooms but also being awestruck with new spiritual birth in adults.

I attended the daylong labor of my eldest daughter and ached for her obvious ordeal. Yet the glowing smile that brightened her exhausted face when Sarah was born helped us all retreat from her mother's pain - as we were washed in the joy of this first grandchild.

As a pastor and counselor, I have also experienced the birth of the seventh or eighth unwanted child to a poverty-stricken woman. I have also encountered the burden of young, frazzled mothers suffering from postpartum depression, unable to tend or attend to their kids. I have stood at the bedside of an alcoholic woman who just delivered an underweight baby suffering from fetal alcohol syndrome. Not all human birth is joyous, especially as we witness the staggering birthrate in third world countries, where women seem to have no choices to speak of, but to submit to their cultures.

Newborns in the spiritual world face daunting obstacles as well. It was a grateful and gracious moment of discovery for me when I learned that the original Aramaic usages of our phrase "born again" could also be translated as "born from above." (John 3:1-21) Nicodemus obviously could not fathom a physical new birth. Jesus had to explain that he had in mind a new spiritual birthing in the Holy Spirit "from above" – a glorious rebirthing from God into an abundant new life, new way, and new truth.

This birth, Jesus went on to explain, is as natural as the wind, yet just as mysterious and unpredictable. I admire Jesus' discernment and skill in diverting Nicodemus and many others from a plodding, literal nailing-down of reality. Jesus refuses to let us manage or manipulate divine reality by the same methods we use to try to control our human world.

In my pastoral work, looking for persons' original, authentic and unique spirits often led me into surprising moments of grace that produced fresh new rebirths of life - in individuals, couples, families and even congregations. Some of these moments came like the wind, sudden, powerful, and unexpected. Yet, at other times blessings happened after we looked and dug for them in predictable and obvious places.

Even when just barely emerging, persons, like freshly unearthed raw gems, will shine and glow on the spot, provided someone is there to help with the digging and polishing. Looking for treasure on home ground often calls for encouragement and nurture.

Blessings, goodness, holiness and love are treasures that are often hidden. However, I believe they are always richly distributed in all life, in all animated beings, divine, human and animal. God's riches are indigenous and inexhaustible. So, my life as counselor and pastor has not only affirmed feelings as essential to natural and healthy emotional lives, but has also celebrated the blessings of nativity – newness of persons. I trust both nature and nativity. They remain for me the dual highway to emotional health and spiritual wealth. I love this highway. It is the route that leads to a higher way of truth and life.

INTRODUCTION:
Core Feelings

—ᴍ—

We come into life unformed, and then we are formed by a shaping process of being informed, and conformed, often becoming deformed and, yearning to be reformed and transformed. When we discover how misshaped our lives are, we long to be re-shaped into our authentic selves. Feelings often go through the same process toward divine reformation and transformation.

I have seen these spiritual blessings as our natural human feelings are dramatically changed into a "new creation" that can only be celebrated as new spiritual realities our of the old emotional malformations – toxic shame healed into humility and self-acceptance, heavy guilt transformed into an ethic of accountability, controlling anger changed into courageous strength, agonizing loneliness into communities of love, aching tiredness refreshed and vitalized, sorrow and sadness becoming profound joy, disabling fear converted into peaceful wisdom, and oppressive pain into sensitive compassion for others. I have been present in the midst of these tranformative rides - as feelings become true friends, redeemed and altered forever by the Holy Spirit. This book is an eyewitness testimony to such miracles of God's healing love.

Like many counselors today, I have concentrated on feelings as essential to a healthy and whole life. To embrace nature and the natural is to also appreciate what were once called our affections. I understand true emotional health and spiritual wealth as natural realities linked together, ready to doubly bless anyone who turns to God for more enrichment and redemption. God makes additions, emendations, alterations and multiplications to our normal, natural capacities to feel.

Nothing seems as native and natural as our basic feelings, which are with us even before birth and are generously included in the core of being until death and beyond. To declare a feeling, we often say we *are* angry, or I *am* angry, describing our entire emotional atmosphere and temperature. It is as if when angry we are feeling that particular feeling all over, deep down and throughout our being. "From nose to toes." We even use the verb "to be" not only to pronounce and announce what we feel but also *who we are* at the moment – angry selves. We find it sensible and natural to say, "I am mad, I am sad, I am glad as easily as we say I feel mad, I feel sad and I feel glad." We find it nonsense to say "I think mad, I think sad or I think glad" without the "I am." We feel feelings, we do not think them. A feeling describes our being from the beginning to the end.

According to Dr. Richard M. Restak in his book "The Infant Mind", Doubleday, 1986, some of the basic emotions expressed and measured on the faces of even newborns are anger, fear, pain, shame and guilt, sadness, distress, disgust, interest, surprise and joy. Crying, which can express many unhappy emotions and smiling, expressing many happy feelings are the two most basic ways to communicate. We change very little from being little. Except that Dr. Restak is certain that infant emotions and facial expressions are much more reliable than adults, who learn to cover up true feelings.

It has been my experience that these basic core feelings fall into two categories: protector feeling and connector feelings. The protector feelings are anger, disgust, contempt, fear, pain, extreme hunger and thirst. Such feeling states are very reactive and immediate. The connector feelings are guilt, shame, loneliness, happiness, pleasure, and satisfaction. Within a year or two, empathy shows up in the baby. These emotional states are more introspective and not quite as reactionary. Protector feelings usually make noise, cry out and are explosive. Connector feelings such as guilt, shame and loneliness are more silent and inward. Even inner happiness, pleasure and satisfaction from a smiling infant connect to the mother or caretaker for more than protection and not just for self. I was amazed to learn that empathy is a basic core feeling. To know that God implants such feeling for others is heartening and wonderful.

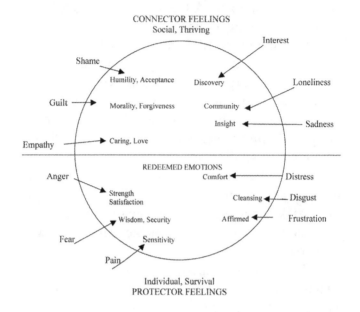

CONNECTOR FEELINGS
Social, Thriving

Interest

Shame

Humility, Acceptance   Discovery   Loneliness

Guilt   Morality, Forgiveness   Community

Insight   Sadness

Empathy   Caring, Love

REDEEMED EMOTIONS

Anger   Comfort   Distress

Strength
Satisfaction   Cleansing   Disgust

Wisdom, Security   Affirmed   Frustration

Fear   Sensitivity

Pain

Individual, Survival
PROTECTOR FEELINGS

I will have a lot to say about feelings in this book. However, I will only share the ones I consider the most basic and common to us all, including the ones studied by Dr. Restak. Nevertheless, there are hundreds of feelings and they all have usually just one word to describe them. Whereas, thoughts usually take more than one word to get the opinion across.

This sharing on "emotional redemption" toward "feeling free" will present only the feelings with which I have the most familiarity - the basic big ones above: anger, fear, pain, shame and guilt, loneliness, sadness, surprise, empathy, satisfaction, comfort and a few more. Love, hope and faith are much more than just feelings. They are divine gifts, much deeper and broader than emotions alone.

As important as feelings are, they are obviously not all that constitute human and divine reality. I do not dare to describe the totality of any such immensities in full or even try to come close. Yet I found this handout below as a partial disclosure, summarizing a portion of my understanding, which I developed and discovered in my ministry, practice and personal life. As you can see, feelings are among the several ways, the main core realities that I believe in.

HOLY HOPE

I am convinced that God never ceases to form, reform, and transform all of creation. I am further assured and reassured that God in Christ works to lift our personal burdens and set us free from the chains that bind us. I therefore believe:

WE ARE RESPONSIBLE.

To the extent that we assume our own responsibility, our serenity and joys increase. This response-ability is ours and belongs to no one else. It is also the basis for our personal morality and social ethic. As God's earthly flock, we are not to be condemned for our natural human weakness, sickness, or waywardness. But we are accountable. We have the choice to be willful or to become willing and allow our divine Shepherd to tend us. We can always turn and return to God for health and salvation. I can express my responsibility and hope in multiple ways.

The first way is spiritual.

God makes no mistakes. I cannot be a mistake, although I make lots of them. I am acceptable with God as the unique person I am, because God fashioned and shaped me. God made me and is not finished with me yet. My uniqueness is not my perfection but my humanity. I am God's imperfect and fallible human being, not merely a human doing. I am also God's child in Christ Jesus by adoption and redeeming grace, as well as God's creation. Since God's creative and redemptive action never ceases, I am a blessed human becoming! Therefore I am loved and precious in God's sight. What more could I need? With the blessing and birthright given me in Christ I have all I need for a whole, wholesome, and holy life.

My birthright is to be who I am today
and no one else.
My blessing is to grow up into the person God
wants me to become.

The second way is emotional.

I can feel. I can only feel feelings. I cannot feel thoughts. Most everyone has a full set of emotions, especially the most useful ones: anger, fear, pain, guilt, shame, loneliness, and many joys. Although I can keep them hidden, doing so would be regrettable, because my feelings can be my friends. All of them reveal more about who I am than all my thoughts, ideas, opinions, or judgments. What I think can often be wrong. Feelings are never right or wrong, they just are. When I discover and uncover my feelings I embrace my most honest reality. Then I can put them to use in appropriate and healthy ways.

The third way is mental.

I can think. I can only think thoughts. I cannot think feelings. I cannot think anger, shame, and loneliness.

However, God gave most of us functional minds and expects us to use them. I can choose the material that my brain entertains, and I can determine how long I dwell on people, places and things. I can use my mind to let others know what I need and want from them. I can, if I so choose, think, speak, and act for myself, without expecting or allowing others to take over that privilege for me.

The fourth way is social.

I can relate. God loves me, and with the love God gives me, I love myself. The love I receive from God is the love that then overflows and touches others. I can give to others the same responsibility and care I assume for myself. However, I can choose not to cripple others by taking over for them. I can change only one person in the world – myself. Expecting others to change is a guaranteed road to disappointment.

I am equal. So are others. When a person is temporarily incapacitated, I can choose, freely, to help. However, I can also choose not to do for another what that person is capable of doing for himself or herself. Relating as "less than" or "more than" is unhealthy and destructive. I have a right to my spiritual, emotional, mental, and physical boundaries. So do others. I have a right not to be abused and live as a victim. I have a duty not to abuse or intrude on others and live as an offender. Whether offended or offending, with God's help I am able, by asking God, to receive the grace of forgiving myself and others of any offense, of making amends and receiving forgiveness. If I choose to commit to loving – first trying to love God with all my heart, soul, mind and strength – then as I gradually learn to love myself and start receiving and feeling God's love, I can begin to hope to love others in the same way.

The fifth way is physical.

I can survive and thrive. I have the right and responsibility for my body, its care and protection. I can decide who, when, where, and how I will be touched. My boundaries are always *only* my business. I will provide a healthy, clean, and pleasing home for my body. I will provide myself adequate food, shelter, rest, exercise, recreation, and clothing. Today's life-giving recovery programs use simple slogans that can be a great help to any one among us who is in a crunch, stuck, feeling hopeless and helpless. I can choose to use these slogans to help me reclaim my holy hope. *Let go and Let God - Live and Let Live - Live One Day at a Time*

***

This book is a mixture of professional and personal experiences. Each chapter blends both parts of my life and history. Some sharings are mostly professional, yet all are autobiographical and authentic. This is my story from where I stand today at age 73. In God's merciful plan, *who I am* has marvelously mattered to some very precious persons along the way. I am grateful God has used me in spite of myself. As you read on, you will not find this not a modest statement but a true one.

From the first chapter on *"From Anger to Courage"* to the last chapter on *"From Desire to Fulfillment,"* you will discover my discoveries. These are, among other things, about the natural and the native, about the now, the next and the new, about formation: un-formation, information, conformation, deformation, reformation and transformation, about uncovery, discovery and recovery, about remembering, religion and spirituality, about individual integrity and equality, about health, wholeness and holiness, freedom and grace, the false and the true, the image of God, choice and control, boundaries and hula hoops, selfishness and serenity, grief and gratitude, love, honor and cherishing, surprise and surrender and, of course, feelings. You will even encounter quite a few interesting animals, friends, counselees, and relatives. Above all, I pray you will come to find what I found - emotional redemption.

Easter, 2004

CHAPTER ONE

From Anger to Courage

—ɯ—

"A person who is angry on the right grounds, against the right persons, in the right manner, at the right moment, and for the right length of time deserves great praise." This comment was seen on the cover of a book, since lost. What is the "right" of anger? Most of us, who have been the target of hostility, find it anything but right. It feels all wrong. In recovery, we are cautioned to avoid "hunger, anger, loneliness and tiredness" as disruptions of our recovery walk. I think I can manage to avoid being hungry, lonely or tired, but how to avoid anger? Should we?

Someone once said, "Anger is a divinely implanted emotion. Closely allied to our instinct for right, it is designed to be used for constructive spiritual purposes. The person who cannot feel anger at evil is a person who lacks enthusiasm for good."

I have observed and experienced the benefits of healthy anger, providing energy to protest injustice and to right wrongs. Perhaps such a dynamic is not anger at all, but determination, courage and resolution to put things right. In my experience if we embrace what we call, anger before it becomes rage and hatred; we can harness this power for good and constructive purposes. Therefore, I find that anger has a valuable gift in its protest-energy against evil, sickness and sin. I recall that Jesus was angry frequently and I am sure it was for all the right reasons.

There is something about righteous indignation that provides strength to combat the unacceptable and unjust things and people of this world. Surely, anger never arises out of trivial matters, but always about something vitally important. I guess if we did not have good, God-given anger, we would be passive, timid and unable to get steamed up about anything worthwhile.

The Wolf Man of the Brazos

While I was in clinical training at the Austin State Hospital, there was a story about a man who was raised by wolves in East Texas. He had been discovered and captured near the banks of the Brazos River. I had read of a similar occurrence in Roman history with the legend of Romulus and Remus. I had also grown up reading about Mowgli and his wolf clan family in Kipling's *Jungle Book*. Surely, these were fictional stories.

My good friend and fellow intern, Jerry Buffington, was as fascinated as I, and we decided to investigate this bizarre tale of a real wolf person.

We heard that when he was first captured as a child, he could not talk or regulate his bodily functions, walked on all fours, and acted like a wild animal. After he was taken into care, he never showed any human inclinations to be civilized. For years, we were told; he had been chained in front of the then "Insane Asylum" as a curiosity and freak show, taunted and teased by passers-by.

To our astonishment, we discovered that he was still a patient at the hospital, some forty years later. He occupied a cell, really more like a cage, where he lived worse than a zoo animal and received scant attention. He had no human interaction except to see his food and water passed to him under his cage door. Weekly, we were told, he was chained in his cell while the floor was hosed down to clean up his excrement, urine, and pieces of uneaten food. Jerry and I were stunned, horrified even, to learn of such a state of affairs. We were also told that we could go to see him if we chose. We jumped at the chance.

As young chaplain-interns, we were out to save the world. We had already volunteered to see patients whom the doctors called "vegetables," making a few surprising discoveries and believing we might have seen some slight improvements in the condition of some as a result of our contacts. Nevertheless, we had never heard anyone referred to as an "animal," especially in this new modern hospital, no longer called an "insane asylum. With bravado and some trepidation, we found a time to go see this alleged man-beast.

Jerry and I set out on a stifling July day to visit the ward where our subject lived—a two-story stucco building with no air conditioning. After being allowed inside by an attendant, who seemed puzzled that two chaplains were coming to call, we entered a dark hall and were overwhelmed by the stench. We said we would like to visit the patients on the second floor. He guided us up the stairs, and immediately we came face-to-face with the cage and the infamous wolf-man. We peered through the bars to see a pitiful unclothed human being, crouched in the corner, who began to tremble at the sight of us. His eyes grew wide, full of fear, and he turned away from us. We tried to communicate with him in calm, soft voices. We prayed. Nothing. He never responded. Jerry and I felt drained, defeated and disgusted at the same time.

We visited some more patients in an open room, which was airy though extremely hot. Each patient we greeted returned our pastoral pleasantries, but I could not make myself present to them. I was still recoiling inside from the wrenching encounter with the man in the cage. As we walked down the stairs to the bright and free outside lawn, I felt an enormous anger and confusion, a desire to shout out my protest to heaven and against the world. My outrage was almost uncontrollable. I asked Jerry how he felt and he said, "Sick." However, I had gone beyond sickness, seized by greater anger than I ever felt in my young life. This was so upsetting that my supervisor had real concern for my stability, considering my father's history. I managed to recover. Yet, forty years later, I still can feel that anger and disgust rising again.

No one could verify the legend of wolves actually raising this pitiful person. His past was less compelling to me than the horrifying present. Therefore, the details of his story seemed irrelevant. What was real to me was the treatment and condition of this so-called patient. Whatever brought him to this place and state of life was not as important as the obvious indignity and low estate of this child of God. This was unacceptable to me.

I tried to make sense of this experience. At chapel, I preached about it, but I had difficulty expressing my anger and angst. Sadness, sorrow, grief, and a great sense of wrong pervaded my spirit. In that particular sermon, I could proclaim no good news, although I went through the motions and declared that God could and would redeem even the worst situations. That, of course, is good news indeed and the cross and resurrection always proclaims the best of news.

Nevertheless, my heart was not in the message. There seemed to be a hole in it. Why was I so overcome with anger? What is it that cries out so loudly when a human being is so diminished and degraded? Why were the hundreds of followers, who loved Jesus, not enraged at his mistreatment and degradation? Apparently, shock and fear had covered any anger they had.

Thinking more of the wolf man than Jesus, I was reminded of a cruel monarch and not the innocent Lamb of God. I began to consider the picture of the great king Nebuchadnezzar, in the book of Daniel, whose mind was changed from a man's to that of a beast. He was driven from among men, made to dwell with the beasts of the field, eating grass like an ox. His body was wet with the dew of heaven until his hair grew as long as eagles' feathers, and his nails were like birds' claws (Daniel 4: 12-33). Apparently, the biblical witness considered the king's punishment to be the ultimate indignity.

Seeing such a degraded and defeated person was revolting and repugnant to me. I saw a potential king in the man in that cage, for he was a person, not a wolf. The Bible's good news was that the king recovered. At Austin State Hospital, the bad news was that this tortured human being died in the same sad state in which as he was found on the riverbank so many years before. This man was never a beast who could be restored to his human state, like the prince in *Beauty and the Beast*. He was a human tragedy and a mystery at the same time.

Nor was this suffering man the first human being to be treated like an animal or worse. Too many human beings—and even one is too many—have been so treated. Too many died in the ovens of the Holocaust. Too many were slaughtered in the killing fields of Cambodia, Bosnia, Kosovo, Africa, and Juarez, Mexico. In our own country, we seldom consider how brutal we were to Native Americans from Christopher Columbus on. Each Indian Reservation is a stark reminder of our cruelty and disrespect to the indigenous population of this continent, including South and Central America.

How can human beings be so inhumane? I can think of no animal species that treats other animals with such enormous cruelty and in such murderous numbers. Where will all this hatred and rage finally take us? When I met the so-called wolf-man, I did not understand my own anger and potential rage. Today, I think I do.

This early experience as a hospital chaplain has blessed me and helped motivate me to do what I can, where I can, to help others deal with anger since I have had to understand and deal with my own. Without a doubt, the major learning about my own anger was "there but for the grace of God, go I." The wolf man could have been me. So could the other patients in the hospital, the cruel conquistadors and Indian fighters, along with the slavers and abusers – all could have been me. Knowing this, that we all have this capacity to harm and hurt others, have made me that much more careful about the enormous power anger has.

I have conducted more workshops on anger management than any other human reality. I like to think I have made a small contribution in staving off domestic family killing fields, by passing on some hard-earned knowledge about anger. What follows reflects some of what I have learned and shared.

Anger: Friend or Foe?

What is anger? It is a subjective, physiological, and emotional reaction, causing an energy flow, rather as electricity can be low or high voltage. Sometimes we have only mild irritation that merely "glows," while at other times we may have an overload of rage that can "blow our fuses" or damage others as well. The anger response comes from our fight-or-flight reactions in our brainstems or limbic system. Fight is experienced primarily as anger, while flight is mostly felt as fear.

Why do we have anger? Like all of our emotions, it has a purpose. Like fear, it is a protector feeling. Anger's purposes are self-protection and self-empowerment, stimulation to solve problems, motivation to right wrongs. Anger energy demands satisfaction and strengthens us to settle conflicts and problems. Healthy and benign anger energy strives for settlement and works for peace through approach rather than avoidance. Anger supports our desires for relief from the problem, rousing us to face and confront disturbing issues, The word "confront" comes from two Latin words that mean "up front, face to face with." Anger helps us face the music and gives us the blessing of assertiveness.

When do we have anger? When something is vitally important to us and we cannot just ignore it or the situation. We can ignore only things that seem trivial and unimportant to us. Our anger ignites to help us deal with moments of perceived threat and loss. Anger also operates in displeasing, unacceptable situations. Surprisingly – and of great importance in working with relationships- anger can sometimes be a defense to cover up other uncomfortable feelings (fear, pain, guilt, shame, or disgust).

Disappointments, frustrations, humiliations, personal attacks and insults (verbal or physical) often set our anger energy in motion. We have anger as often as we find anything that is not right. Problems trigger it. Conflicts trigger it. Anger is usually normally about injustice. Its existence is always a normal reaction and therefore legitimate, if we are reading the situation accurately.

Unfortunately, some of us do not perceive reality and are reacting to delusions and deceptions. To pick up a stick to ward off an imaginary bear is understandable, once we know what is being seen and heard. Perhaps too much of our anger is like that, warding off imaginary hallucinations of reality, which are not there. These are not warranted because they are unreal. The anger may be valid if you grant the illusion. Illusions are dangerous. Paranoia is dangerous.

Believing his fantasy that I was a threat to his marriage, a former counselee threatened me. He told me he had a gun loaded for my death, and he soon found himself questioned by the police as a result of his threats. Thank God he soon moved out of the country and getting well. One of my colleagues had his tires slashed by a paranoid patient. Many doctors and other helping professionals are victims of those who accuse them of fictitious wrongs.

Whether anger particulars are illusory or real, the misguided approaches of saying, "Don't be angry" or encouraging someone to stifle and stuff anger will not work. Therefore, anger, like any feeling, depends on many events, happenings, or other situations. It is dependent upon these causes—not independent in and of itself. When we are put down, demeaned, or shamed in any way, anger must result, whether it is acknowledged or not. It is a reactive effect, not an origin nor a source in itself. Anger is always derivative. It derives from what we see, hear, and think, whether accurate or distorted. Anger itself does not know if our data is correct or not. It takes us as we are and without any benefit of doubt. Anger does not think; it reacts. Like a computer, what goes in comes out. Good stuff or garbage. It makes no judgments.

Is anger morally bad? No. Is it morally good? No. Anger, like any feeling, is neither good nor bad. It just is. We cannot help having it. Then what is wrong with anger? The wrongness arises when someone has too much or too little anger and uses that anger in unhealthy, hostile, unproductive, even destructive ways. Anger comes in degrees and can be misused and misdirected. The feeling itself is not wrong. The behavior we choose to express it can be very wrong. We can underuse anger, or we can overuse it.

Too much anger energy we call rage, and rage constitutes a major social problem. Today we are witnessing the dangers of road rage. When anger turns to rage, we become stupid. Doctors I have known maintain that our brains become oxygen-depleted, because blood rushes to our arms and legs for "fight/ flight," and we find it hard to think straight. Some people experience "seeing red" and become out of control. That is why the conventional strategies of counting to ten and taking deep breaths work. I have heard medical men also say that such calming and breathing tactics really do help us in getting oxygen back into the brain. Only when we are able to think again can we respond constructively.

Someone with too little anger energy presents weakness and vulnerability. If our protest response never rises above a low level, we find ourselves subjected to abuse, becoming doormats for other people. Anger is useful and good when it enables us to assert ourselves, face up to threats, and protect ourselves with appropriate boundaries to fortify our rights. Anger energy produces manageable strength so long as the anger remains within controllable limits. It is our choice and no one else's.

We can choose our behavior? Yes, indeed. Even more surprising, we can also choose our thoughts and our wants, in addition to choosing our actions. We cannot choose not to have feelings, including anger. All feelings are emotional reactions to our other primary realities. Then can we control our feelings? You bet! We do it by using the freedom we have to shape our primary reality (our perceptions, thoughts, wants, and our actions). That's how feelings are managed and regulated—by becoming aware of what we perceive and by choosing what we think, what we desire, and what we do .The most crucial influence is our thinking, which mostly determines how we use or misuse our feelings. Feelings are meant to serve, not master us.

The best way to think of anger is this: Am I using my anger energy FOR or AGAINST? Another way to approach the matter would be to consider what the anger is protesting, reflect on the anger-issue, and then thoughtfully choose to use that anger energy FOR the self and others. As a Christian, I would modify the saying of personal choice to "If it is to be, it is up to me and thee, Lord." Dealing with anything as powerful and as useful as anger needs divine assistance.

Anger management needs all the help it can get.

Anger FOR myself and with God is resolute courage and determination.

Anger FOR and WITH others and God is mutual encouragement and fortitude.

Anger AGAINST myself and without God is shamefulness and self-loathing.

Anger AGAINST others and without God's help is belligerence and hostility.

Even three years after suicide bombers rammed the Trade Center Towers and the Pentagon I still am in a lingering shock and reaction to this disaster and the unholy evil of it. In the midst of all the innocent lives snuffed out and families rent asunder – I was impressed by the immediate automatic replies. These seemed to be anger reactions *against* others with extreme belligerence and hostility, calling for revenge, then some few reactions against self, full of shamefulness and self-loathing for our mistaken foreign policy. I recognized this is anger without God. Then very soon after the initial calls for retaliation came anger *for* self and others with God that spoke of courage and determination, encouragement and fortitude. Our leaders looked to God to redeem our outrage and search for justice with divine aid, transforming our energies to love for innocent life everywhere. We were called to the preservation of freedom and to the making of peace and sharing of love.

The Wall Street Journal even called for bombing our enemies with grain, medical supplies and food. Righteous indignation within God's righteousness looks for good outcomes and solutions provide benefits to humankind. Such indignation without help from our Lord produces more violence and destruction. I give thanks for the thoughtfulness going on within the hearts and souls of love in America today

A good example of how anger can be transformed from rage and hate to a new kind of strength and love in one person's life, who turned to God for help is this story of Roger.

Roger's Rage

A few years ago, I was called by a law enforcement agency to counsel an officer who had come close to committing "over-reactive" actions towards citizens. His career was in jeopardy. Roger was a conscientious professional who could not control his anger. He had been reprimanded several times for over-zealous behavior. I agreed to work with him.

Little did Roger's superiors know! He shared with me that not only did he throw his weight around on duty, but also frequently "lost it" – his self-control – when off duty. He admitted to carrying his automatic weapon and badge with him when out of uniform, and had twice terrorized his wife and three children when driving on the freeway. On both occasions when a driver had either cut him off or honked at him, he pursued those he perceived as culprits, ran them on to the shoulder of the road, drew his gun, pointed it in their faces as he "badged" them and "chewed them out" threatening to arrest them.

These incidents were never reported. Roger should have been relieved of duty or dismissed. Yet, these incidents did not lead to lawsuits or jail. It was all I could do to remain in a confidential relationship with Roger when he told me this. If I were his superior and knew of these incidents, he would have been fired on the spot. Fortunately, someone in a supervisory position to him saw that he needed help and wanted him to get it before something drastic occurred.

I could see that Roger was truly remorseful, scared and more than eager to get his anger under control. He found what I had learned about anger to be helpful and hopeful, especially that he had "choices." Furthermore, he discovered that suppressing anger makes it worse, while embracing it and using it for constructive purposes is possible. After several sessions of working on the issues underlying his rage attacks, we began to practice creative anger. He learned to talk about the problems and look for solutions, rather than move so quickly into his "fight" reaction. He practiced thinking and responding, not allowing himself to be the victim of unthinking macho-ness.

We began our sessions by "thingafying" his anger monster as an "it" that did not reflect his true self. I explained that I believed that things that happen are just that – things and happenings – that are not persons. I invited him to name this furious rage and he chose the name "Flaming Fury." I asked him if he thought these rage attacks belonged to him and whether he was willing to lay claim to them as his own. "I hate them!" he protested. He wanted to give up all claims to such misery.

We then began to entertain the notion that these terrible spells were rather like demonic possession that took control of his real personality, his God-created self. So, we externalized his rages, gave a depersonalized name to them and began talking about each episode as if "Flaming Fury" was not only out to get others but to embarrass, threaten and even ruin him – Roger – as a person.

I had a strong suspicion that Roger's demon was his father, who was probably a rage addict himself. Since children learn what they live, such patterns of controlling rage make sense. Yet, when the purpose of control and strength is no longer needed, the anger energy can be released. Then, more productive ways of achieving results can be chosen, such as - talking. We did not stay together long enough to confirm his father's teaching role. Nevertheless, I knew that Roger wanted to reject the ways of raging. It was destroying him.

By looking at "Flaming Fury" as alien and unwanted, we spent several sessions teaming up against this terrible force. There was no question that this form of anger was working against him and others. Together we saw how this coercive evil attacked and controlled him, creating hostility and belligerence in a potentially peaceful man. I gave him a worksheet to fill out that asked him to outline how this raging inter-loper had influenced his life and affected his feeling, thinking, view of himself, relationships and overall behavior. After filling out his form, we both agreed that his nemesis had nothing good in mind for him at all. We set out to outwit "Flaming Fury."

We first spent some time figuring out the monster's trickery, its nature, its purposes and what other forces reinforced and teamed up with it to make things worse. He discovered that he was being lied to, dealing with a cunning adversary who could cause him to indulge in childish tantrums, entranced him with his own power and influence as a lawman by appealing him to catching the criminal drivers, and gave him perceived justification for pursuing offenders anywhere.

I asked if he knew that Satan was called the "father of lies, the adversary and great deceiver." He agreed that he felt confused and under attack. He began to think he was indeed the victim of a great deception that could destroy him. I reminded him of the Gospel account, how Satan lied to Jesus and tempted him with similar deceptions for power and control. (Matthew 4:11) He did not want to consider that the Prince of Darkness was after him, nor did I. However, a temporary consideration of that possibility made great sense to him.

A Bible-centered Christian deacon, Roger began to see his predicament as spiritual warfare, and we both began to lay plans to use the higher power of Jesus and his Word and Presence to combat the enemy. I reminded him that Jesus asked the demonic powers in Mark 5:1-20 what their names were before he cast them out. He saw we were doing the same thing. We searched the Scripture, prayed together and became prayer warriors to gang up with the Lord against "Flaming Fury." Prayer also became a time to breathe, center and slow down the reactionary instincts, and get oxygen to the brain.

When Roger consciously and intentionally turned his life and will over to the benign influence and holiness of Jesus Christ, he discovered and instituted all sorts of new ways, new plans and new thoughts to employ his "spiritual troops" against the foe. One of the first and most sensible moves Roger made was to leave his gun and badge at home for they were being subverted and misused by the hated enemy against him. Without his symbols of authority, he was less menacing. Then he began to find ways to drive on the freeways in peace, to think of his role as a "peace officer" – to make peace not wage war – and to consider his precious family's safety. His most admirable change was to invite his wife to drive! What a stretch for a macho man to make! This was one of the most remarkable "emotional redemptions" I have ever witnessed.

He began to invite his more tender and gentle feelings into life, and became more mature, peaceful and joyful. "I feel like the real me" he exclaimed. He felt a new strength with his redeemed anger. Roger became so articulate about anger that he began to teach a Sunday School class on "battling the beasts of rage" and had the most popular class in his church. This success continued as he reached outside his church to teach a course to recruits on anger management and has even begun to talk to gangs, students in school and anyone else who would listen to him about "attacking the problems, not the persons." Needless to say, he has been promoted. I am also glad to say that Roger has become one of the best examples of a peaceful and productive teacher on anger issues in the community. When one has to learn, one of the best ways to accomplish that is to teach.

I am proud of Roger, who is a living example of talking over anger issues instead of acting them out. The old and out-of-date advice of "shouting, punching, chopping wood, digging weeds and expressing anger" is a classic failure. Such old ideas make it worse for most. Talking and understanding what problems underlie the anger energy is the process of redemption. Seeking solutions does work and is *working wonders* in courageous Roger.

The Scripture Roger chose for the dashboard of his cars was *"Be angry but do not sin; do not let the sun go down on your anger."* (Ephesians 4:26.2)

Questions to ponder:

1. Did the members of your own family of origin provide useful or unhelpful models for dealing with anger? Was God ever more than a curse word? When and where?

2. How do you allow yourself to feel and express anger? Do you fight, or flee? Do you stifle and stuff it, become extremely angry, or talk it through calmly? When you are angry do you ever say or do things you later regret? Can Jesus teach anything about anger and honesty?

3. Can you describe and locate the bodily sensations you experience when you are angry? Some of us who have never allowed ourselves to feel our anger do not even know how it feels. Give yourself permission to name the places where your body experiences the anger.

4. How do you respond when someone close to you is feeling anger toward you? Are you able to talk about it with that person? If not, can you pray for patience, guidance and new responses?

5. When you feel anger toward another person, are you able to ask that person to listen to what you have to say? Can you say so without blaming the person? Can you pray and ask for solution for both, not self-justification?

6. If anger is a problem for you, whom might you ask to help you? There are many good books and good people who have learned how to be strong without hostility. Try Al-Anon, CODA, or a Prayer Group and offer it all up to God.

CHAPTER TWO

From Fear to Wisdom

—m—

*Jesus said to the twelve, "Do you wish also to go
away?" Simon Peter answered him, "lord to whom
will we go? You have the words of eternal life; and
we have believed, and have come to know, that you
are the Holy One of God."* John 6:69

That's what panicked St. Peter. Jesus had the words.
The words of eternal life, or complete safety and
security ... or, as we say in church, *salvation.* Peter
knew as we do, we have no other viable choice. To
whom can we turn for salvation except Jesus? We try
other saviors, of course. Who else is "the Holy One of
God?" Peter could trust, though at times, completely
misunderstand the words of Jesus, but he could
always trust his Master, even, as we know, he could
hardly trust himself. We too, know we are undepend-
able and quite insecure in our own untrustworthiness.
Fortunately, God in Christ does not just come and go,

and come to our aid at only certain special times. He is always in the driver's seat.

I remember how safe I used to feel asleep in the back seat as my parents drove us all safely home. It is the same with our faith and trust in God. The sooner we let him take the wheel as we in the back seat, even asleep, unaware of his route, speed, and manner of driving...not knowing or understanding even how to drive, the sooner he will take care of us and get us where we need to be...safe and sound.

Our life in Christ is not to drive, but to be trusting passengers on the Ark of Salvation, and at other times to be members of the crew. One thing is certain; we are not the Captain, nor the first mate, nor any of the officers. Christ and his holy angels are driving, and steering, not us. When we stop straining to run the show, trust him instead and take our places as God's stumbling passengers and bungling crew, we will get our priorities straight and receive his plan of salvation with confidence and child-like faith.

Why? Because our Lord sets us free. Free from what? Fear, mostly, and all that goes with it: paranoia, futility, hostility, despondency, hopelessness, desolation, shamefulness and shamelessness, and blame. Jesus, our deliverer, delivers us from the bondage of all the fears of existence, with his presence. Peter knew that much. He didn't need to figure it all out, and he didn't have to "get it," he could trust the Holy One of God, even when he had no idea what was going on. He knew Jesus was at the wheel and had everything under his control. All Peter needed was Jesus, and there was no way he was going to leave the Lord of Life. Peter knew enough. So do we, we know the same time-tested blessed assurance, tested out on the "proving grounds" of this world's short human history; that is, if we were looking, listening and learning anything at all.

Just think of the chilling apprehension among the disciples and with Peter, when they saw other disciples "jumping ship" and leaving. They heard the same "hard sayings," and could have also begun to doubt their master's sanity. The thought of bailing out and leaving, or of jumping off the train, was even more terrifying. Leaping off a speeding train is pretty close to certain death. That's our choice still - staying on board a fast-moving, mysterious church (the mystical Body of Christ), trusting the journey will be a safe one, the right one or jump. Peter chose the only way. Peter chose the right way. I have often told myself, "You'd better stick with Jesus. He's the only chance in town."

I have a fond memory of a game we played as a child. It's called, "Kick the Can." I don't remember all the details, except when you run and kick the can, you shout something like "Ollie, Ollie, Otts in freed. All come home." I never found out who Ollie was. Well, I didn't "get it" at the time. Like Peter, I just played the game. Well, I discovered later that I had heard it all wrong. There was no Ollie. The words were: "All and All and All SET FREE. All come home." That is the Gospel, and I did not know it. Like Peter, I just stumbled and bungled along, because I did not want to be left out, alone, and scared.

Our freedom is in the Christ, whose love drives out all fear, and who always welcomes us safely home to himself. Whatever suffering we undergo, our glory, safety, joy and love are all in Christ Jesus. That goes for all of us. "All and all and all set free. All come home," Jesus shouts. If we miss his call, when he kicked the can on Calvary, he will still reach out to us in love and ask, "Do you wish to go away?" hoping we will answer with Simon Peter, "Lord, to whom shall we go? You have the words of eternal life, and we have believed, and have come to know, that you are the Holy One of God." We do not have to kick any cans. Coming home to Jesus is free. All we have to do is get up or open our hearts and come home to him and receive the blessing that is always there in his arms for his lost, confused, tired and frightened children.

The Circus Wagon

One of my first memories was eating from a tin "Barnum Animals Crackers" box, painted to resemble a cheerfully colored circus wagon. Nevertheless, that wagon was also a cage. The animals pictured on the outside of the box were majestic, wild, and untamed beasts. They were also behind bars. The cookies inside the box were shaped into believable copies of jungle animals. These were not comic Disney animals with smiling faces and human characteristics. These beasts were the real things. I remember a rhino, a lion, an elephant and a hippo, and they all looked the way wild animals should look. They were just like the animals I had seen at the Bronx Zoo.

Sadness stifled any pleasure I had in eating the cookies or watching the zoo animals, for they were prisoners. This seemed so unnatural, so wrong. Today, when I see animals cooped up or imprisoned, I still experience grief. I find it hard to push this sorrow down; such is my heartache for caged beings, animal or human. Seeing animals in their natural surroundings without barriers or boxes is one of the joys of my life. I hope someday to go on a real safari in Africa or experience the Alaskan wilderness. I know the pure delight I shall feel in watching such unfettered freedom.

Life without barriers has always appealed to me. A zest for emancipation is a powerful part of who I am. Along with this taste for liberty, I have always had an optimistic trust in the true and the authentic in all beings, including us human ones. This belief energizes my life for I have witnessed far too many human imprisonments of the soul.

Most of these incarcerated spirits, through the tyranny of others, have been living lying lives. Facts have been replaced with falsehoods. Personal integrity has been sacrificed upon the altars of compliance. And yet the wonder is that person after person reached out for new life, aching to be the real thing yet not knowing how or even who they are, exhausted with trying to build their lives according to some other person's blueprint.

Seeking genuine selfhood is not easy. Whom do you listen to? What standards of thought and behavior do you accept? How does one distinguish healthy and truthful lessons from all that is unhealthy and incorrect? How shall we discern what is right and what is wrong, know good and bad, separate truth from lies, when all we have to go by is what we have learned from our culture, and our crews? The communities in which we live along with our families can bless as well as curse our inner chambers of the self.

Breaking free from our prisons of inaccuracy and deception is almost impossible without help. So many persons have become delusional, accepting lies as gospel truth, unable to tell the difference. A deluded person never recognizes the delusion until God makes some opening for truth to break through. Such can be the awesome responsibility of the counselor, speaking the life-giving truth in love. With God's help, I have found great joy in being able to help facilitate a few such spiritual jailbreaks toward authenticity. Being an active conspirator in helping others find freedom and genuineness and the living Christ always brings me joy mixed with an awesome and humbling wonder. Like a kid unlocking the cages and letting the prisoners escape, I love it when any being finds new and unexpected freedom and validity in Christ.

Bill's Breakout

Forty-year old Bill certainly lived in a cage, though it had no visible bars. One of my most gratifying experiences was being his accomplice in finding new life and liberty. Bill's major issue was fear.

Fear is a protector feeling. It gives us important messages. Serving as an antenna for danger, fear comes in degrees from anxiety to terror and is proportional to the extent of danger. A yellow caution sign is less urgent than a red flashing railroad-crossing signal. We are born with fear, and in moderate amounts, it is useful. Only when we move on into fear overload do its emotional effects become destructive. The blessings of fear are wisdom, prudence, sensible avoidance and self-protection. The curses of fear are panic, falling apart, weakness and victimhood.

We often think of wild animals as predators or prey. In the animal world, we observe natural instincts to fight, flee, or freeze when in danger. Many animals react to threats by hiding, digging, bristling, or spraying chemical counterattacks. Many human beings react in the same ways.

Bill was counted among the prey. Always on the defensive, he taught himself to become a "freezer"— frozen with fear. He longed to bristle and spray. He dreamed of fighting back, but he found such displays of standing up for himself swiftly swept aside. So, he became like a rabbit or a mouse, scurrying for protection down some hole. His main instinct was to flee, to escape. He told me often how he really wanted to "get out of town and start a new life away from it all." Yet most of the time he became frozen, unable to fight or flee.

Like an animal caught in the headlights of a car, he was unable to move until he was dumbstruck or even struck down. He could not fight back. Words froze in his throat. To resist or even entertain the idea of defiance was to invite more overwhelming abuse. Often he described his feelings as "being run over by a freight train."

Surprisingly, the major instigators of his fear were his bedridden mother, closely followed by his elder sister. This duo dominated his life so completely that he did not know how to do anything but serve, help, care-take, and agree. He perfected the roles of chauffeur, cook, waiter, nurse, housekeeper, and servant to the two women. Sadly, he found a strange kind of security in accepting this process, fitting into their mold.

They were the only family he had. His father died when he was seven. He was left alone with "his" two ladies. Knowing no other way, he accommodated and acquiesced. To Bill, it seemed only right to assume personal responsibility for meeting their demands. They were in charge, and he thought he believed in their commands. He felt guilty when he did not live up to their unreasonable expectations. Trying ever harder to please, he failed.

Rarely did Bill think of himself as important or worthy, except as the direct reflection of what was expected even as the expectations kept growing. Eventually he could not remember a time when he had performed adequately in anyone's eyes, including his own. Guilt and shame became his daily companions. "I can never do anything right [toxic guilt] so there must be something wrong with me [shamefulness]." That sentence became his habitual lament.

Seldom have I known a man so imprisoned in a cage of perceived inadequacy. When I first met Bill, he was pitiful and beaten down. His human dignity was so diminished that I thought caged animals retained more self-respect. Where did he find the courage to come and see me for help? The pain he was experiencing must have been so great that he could no longer ignore it. Asking for assistance is the first; the hardest step in gaining liberty and release. Yet, the journey to freedom begins with that first step.

How did Bill escape? By discovering his true God-given self, which became his new self. Bill's authentic being had hidden and completely covered. He found that his habitual frozenness was false. It was a bad habit he had learned from others. Earnie Larsen defines unhealthy habits as "self-destructive learned behaviors" and Bill was an excellent learner. If he could learn self-damaging conduct, he could also do the opposite and learn, with God's grace and assistance to thaw out, letting his own healthy nature emerge.

First, he was able to accept the fact that he was not a born fighter. Second, once he accepted that his authentic life and style spontaneously impelled him to back off and flee, he began to trust and practice his innate defensive shiftiness. He started welcoming his capacity to be fast on his feet. He found that avoidance, stealth, and cunning could serve him well as he began to outmaneuver his jailers. At least for a while, Bill embraced what he had always thought was weakness and timidity. He adopted a manner of life based on his own free choices, instead of being compelled by others, choosing to make necessity into a virtue. He learned to love the role of the cagey convict who accepts his cage of imprisonment—for the time being. He started to make his incarceration work for him as he worked his way around his mother and sisters in new and creative ways. His fear began to become transformed into new wisdom.

This new role touched his soul in such a profound way that he told me, "This is my true self, and I love it! It feels so right and so new!" Such a statement reminded me of the part in our Holy Communion which exclaims: "Let us give thanks to the Lord. It is *right* to give him thanks and praise [emphasis mine]." In older services, it has the phrase: "It is *meet and right* so to do." I like the older version better. "Meet and right" means "fitting and proper." Bill was meeting his real self and this was proper, appropriate and genuine. He had finally made the right fit and felt just right for the first time. Bill's fear was redeemed, changed into caution and care for himself. His anxiety led him to wisdom.

To meet your true self is one of life's greatest joys. Bill conjured up Goldilocks for me, as she found her own special and correct porridge. When any of us can be "face to face" with our own souls and see the right and real person looking back at us, the event is rare and wondrous. Bill is now wearing his own uniform and it fits him to a T.

There is an old saying in sports: "Age, cunning, deceit and treachery can defeat youth and skill." Bill stopped working harder and gleefully took on the job of working smarter. Like a boxer against a slugger, he could not overcome his prison guards, but he could outdance and outwit them. Soon he claimed and savored every moment of freedom he could find. Both of us delighted in this newly created busy and brilliant Bill. He was no longer frozen but burning with a blistering charm and good humor. The old matriarchal rules were being broken. Before long, each time we met, the two of us were exulting in the wily ways of William. I usually began our sessions with a playful question: "What win has wise William won this week?"

As time passed, this newly chosen self seemed so true and real that Bill regained a natural dignity that felt God-given to him. So it seemed to me. Being made in the image of God, we agreed, was not only being *like* God but being *as God likes us to be*. God creates each one of us as special and unique. We are cherished as an image in the painter's eye and imagination long before the brush is put to canvas.

The selves God creates are our true and real selves, yet we drift far away from those originals. Like the jungle animals once roaming free and now confined to a constricting cage, we learn to live false and unreal lives, losing sight of who we are meant to be. In every generation, God's good beginnings are soon covered over with false images and distressingly inauthentic versions of what it means to be fully human, fully alive.

There are at least two sides of "image"...the godlike qualities he provided us that are comparable to the divine plus the special unique way he sculpted each soul's distinctive uniqueness. It is a double wonder - our way of becoming. We were imaged as art treasures formed by the master artist, reflecting the creator but also expressing our own inner beauty. A popular song from the seventies sang, "Everyone is beautiful in their own way."

Unfortunately, even the most gorgeous gardens can become infested with pests and enemies who see only a feast for their evil appetite. Therefore, what were once our natural human natures become our caged constricted human natures—our fallen victimized natures.

Victims fall quite easily and painfully. Each person is born into a Garden of Eden, which already contains evil. Falling and failing become common when our family and communal serpents begin their control and influence over us. In that sense, Bill and I came to see, that original sin is still alive and powerful within our family gardens. Such evil originates early on.

The beginnings of neglect, ridicule and abuse in our human environments come from some source outside ourselves. Simple cause-and-effect leads us to ask "Where, when, how and why did we become damaged goods?" Original perpetrators are as real as original victims. All our gardens begin with our birth and with our first learnings. We are not born into vacuums but into gardens that often seem like jungles. These are our families and our communities, where our tutors teach us.

Yet, original righteousness is also alive and just waiting to be resurrected in these same jungle-like gardens. We can also share in our biblical parents' triumph. Redemption, rebuilding, renewal, refreshment can all revitalize our soil and our plants.

Pestilence does not have to rule or become a permanent inhabitant. The true God-made garden is still there, covered up by layered accretions of unhealthy happenings, plagues and disasters that simply happen and cannot be avoided.

These happenings take place as vulnerable persons are stigmatized, traumatized and victimized from infancy on. Such stigma, trauma and victimization come from without not within. Extreme abuse sometimes brutalizes victims into becoming brutal as well. Far too often, the beaten child becomes the child-beater. Not all our households are safe, secure and loving environments. Not all our schools provide consistent affirmation and approval. Not all our clubs, societies, colleges, groups or neighborhoods are benign and caring. Bullies and brutes find their victims. Every day innocent persons are crushed, physically and spiritually, by perpetrators and persecutors who seem to find gratification and delight in demeaning and even destroying those who are different, using and abusing them for their own selfish satisfactions.

Bill soon stopped accepting victimhood to embrace sonship. This was his choice. He would refuse to serve coercion. Victim no longer fit. It can no longer define him. Child of God and Member of Christ are "meet and right" for him now. The false Bill found the true Bill as he began his search for the true image by which the divine artist defined him, having known Bill, as the prophet Jeremiah tells us, "while he was still in his mother's womb." (Jeremiah 1:5)

Now Bill's self-search has expanded into a greater awareness of the real Maker and Shaper of his life.

Neither Bill nor I was satisfied with *mere* nature. We both conspired to find *super* nature and the supernatural gift of the God of Bill's understanding. Bill has been a Christian believer from childhood, so to him it made sense and showed respect for his own faith community that we should search out a scripture from the Christian tradition that would express and confirm his experience of spiritual rebirth. Best of all, Bill had stopped trying to manage it on his own. He had found a teammate. Consequently, I introduced him to God-management instead of self-help and control. Together, this is what we found:

> *"Now the Lord is the Spirit, and where the Spirit of the Lord is, there is freedom. And all of us with unveiled faces, seeing the glory of the Lord as though reflected in a mirror, are being transformed into the same image from one degree of glory to another; for this comes from the Lord, the Spirit."* (2 Corinthians: 3:17-18)

Bill still takes delight in fulfilling his role of Wily William, the blessed stage self he has uncovered to replace his former cursed self. In reality, he is gentle, kind, and naturally pleasing. He pulls off his new act with genuine charm and confidence. This role is real, delighting his friends and confounding his old jailers, who have lost their power over him. Everyone acknowledges the miracle being wrought in this former timid, cowed person.

I believe Bill found strength for his journey at first in the powerful Twelve-Step motto, "Fake it till you make it." Now, without a doubt, Bill is making it with no fakery at all. He makes choices, instead of allowing himself to be coerced. He is practicing *responses* with thoughtful actions and words, rather than *reacting* by freezing up. Whenever he feels the freezing coming on, he allows himself time to think, pray, and plan his next word and next step with a new routine, according to God's script.

Now that fear no longer paralyzes him, he has even learned to *float and to flow* with the tides of life each day. He uses his anxiety for prudence and caution, as a natural signal of the possible danger of "headlights ahead" and oncoming freight trains. He is using his feelings of fear to guide him into watchfulness and wisdom, trusting his native ability to dodge and weave to avoid threats. Like a recovering alcoholic who knows the wisdom of staying out of bars, Bill now seeks out the safe places and safe people in his world.

Finding new playmates and playgrounds, he now goes bowling weekly. He has joined a new spirit-filled church. He attends a Twelve-Step meeting devoted to liberating relationships, called Codependents Anonymous. He has begun a new business. He has made new friends, male and female, without checking his choices out with anyone but God.

One day Bill shared a wild thought that if he were an animal he would be a coyote! Known as an escape artist, this animal is wily, clever, resourceful, persistent and irrepressible. Native Americans respect the coyote as the "Trickster." I rejoiced with Bill's insight. He was reveling in being a coyote and welcoming this spirit of escape and cleverness to keep on liberating his life.

He has begun his escape. He has broken out and is over the wall. The escape plan was there all the time. We uncovered it together, yet he did most of the digging. Bill's new freedom still feels strange and unfamiliar to him at times, but he refuses to go back into his old prison. Now his fear has a purpose— providing preventive and precautionary wake-up calls. The fear energy is now experienced as excitement for the next adventure, instead of the anxiety that kept him stuck and frozen. His fear has somewhere to go now—taking him out of harm's way and into God's realm.

Did Bill get out of town? Not yet. Not physically. He no longer needs a geographic cure. He is already free, free to be, free to become, and free to believe in the self he has found directly reflected to him from his divine source of meaning.

Throughout our journey together, I encouraged Bill by taking an old advertising slogan, "The best revenge is *living* well" and changing it to "The best revenge is to *be* well" meaning no revenge at all. The way to accomplish this non-revenge revenge was to stop looking to "his" women as his *de facto* goddesses, his only source of life and meaning. His real source of wellness is the well of Christ and his living water.

Now he takes his thirst for identity and communion to a healthy and saving source. Bill is discovering that any revenge belongs only to God, whose revenge is love. He knows that as he is filled and refreshed by our Lord he will no longer live as a victim and can help set his former perpetrators free as well.

Bill's women and I have never met. If I were to meet them, I am sure I would find sincere and pleasant people, who have no idea of their role as offenders and abusers. I am also sure they would never consider themselves as powerful as goddesses. My prayer is that they too will become free and authentic and escape their imprisonment. I also pray God will intervene in their lives, bringing them more joy and love, redemption and renewal, just as has happened in Bill's life.

Today Bill trusts in a trustworthy God to love him, bless him, and keep him in his current state of being well—staying open to any major repairs that may become necessary in the future. The next time we meet, I am sure he will have many answers to my greeting, "what's new?"

During Bill's therapy and inspired by his recovery I put together this chart of the self's journey, adapted from Donald R. Hands and Wayne L. Fehr's helpful book, "Spiritual Wholeness for Clergy," (Alban Institute, 1993), page 33. The biological journey is one of steady growth to midlife and then steady decline as we age until physical death. However, spiritually we enter life with an innocent and pure self that may decline due to trauma, abuse and stigma and find ourselves a dishonored false self. At the moment of truth, we come to ourselves as prodigals away from our true destiny. With God's help, we turn upward to a life of wholeness and health as we uncover, discovery and recover the selves we were meant to be – our new true selves. If we do not turn upward, we continue on the false self's road to spiritual death, and our souls decline as our physical bodies do. Millions who "hit bottom" and began a newer and truer pilgrimage to God have attested to this road to recovery.

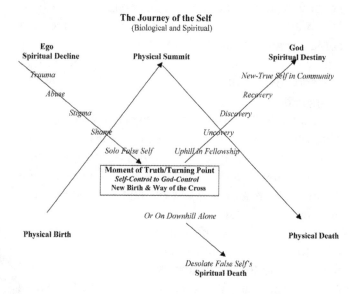

The Journey of the Self
(Biological and Spiritual)

| Ego | | God |
| Spiritual Decline | Physical Summit | Spiritual Destiny |

Trauma — *New-True Self in Community*

Abuse — *Recovery*

Stigma — *Discovery*

Shame — *Uncovery*

Solo False Self — *Uphill in Fellowship*

Moment of Truth/Turning Point
Self-Control to God-Control
New Birth & Way of the Cross

Or On Downhill Alone

Physical Birth — **Physical Death**

Desolate False Self's
Spiritual Death

Questions to Ponder

1. Is there some person or relationship in my life that feels like a cage? Who or what is it? Does it feel old? Does it feel unnatural? Is God present?

2. If I could break out of that "cage," how might I feel after it happened?
   Would escape feel new? Would it be natural? Will God protect you?

3. What is preventing my breakout from my "cage" and what animal could I be to accomplish my release? A tiger? A deer? A coyote? A lamb?

4. When some interaction with another person makes me afraid, do I freeze and clam up, seek an escape, or stay to talk it through and find something new as well as natural? Is it possible to pray?

5. If I need to break out, can I do it on my own, or might I need "angelic" help? A friend? A counselor? A pastor? A family member? God? A church?

6. If God were to call me by my true name, what would I want that name to be? Would I be willing to change to turn upward with help from a loving fellowship of Christians?

CHAPTER THREE

From Pain to Sensitivity

—〰—

My father was a professional soldier, a West Pointer and an infantry officer. From birth to the age of 12 years, I lived with my parents on Army posts. I was born at Fort Benning, Georgia, and later lived in the Philippines, Hawaii, Alabama, Panama and Washington State on permanent Army forts. My earliest memories were of cannon shots and bugle calls. The wake-up call of "Reveille" each morning and the cannon's roar at the raising of the flag greeted each day. Another cannon blast accompanied the lowering of the flag and the playing of "Retreat" that signaled the end of daylight. I fell asleep listening to the beautiful rendition of the nighttime calls of "Tattoo" soon followed by "Taps." To my young life, "Taps" was my lullaby for pleasant dreams. It was the end of the day, not the end of life. All my waking and sleeping took place within compounds for American military men and their families. The regimented round of scheduled activities was comforting. At night, I could hear the Military Police as they walked their sentry duty outside our quarters. I felt protected and important, comforted and secure. I greeted each new morning with anticipation. Living in hope, I looked forward to days full of play, companionship and discovery.

Seldom did I leave my fortress home to venture into town. Before I entered first grade, the outside world was unknown and unnecessary to me. Each fort was a world unto itself, and each post was pretty much the same. To me, the Army was the civilized world. Everything was provided. Housing, stores, food, recreation, medical care, social life and even chapel were within walking distance. There were kids galore, parks to play in, a huge parade ground to run across, a golf course to explore, stables to hang around, trees to climb, many homes to visit, playgrounds and pools and gyms, all beckoning each day. I loved it. I loved the Army. For me, it was paradise. I was filled with so much ecstatic love for life that I can recall actually hugging a big palm tree in front of my house to express that love. Apparently, tree hugging was an early childhood decision for me.

Although I had never heard of Albert Schweitzer his words from *"Reverence for Life,"* described my feeling: "Reverence for life comprises the whole ethic of love in its deepest and highest sense. It is the source of constant renewal for the individual and for mankind."

Those first dozen years of my life also embraced animals. In the tropics, many homes had monkeys, parrots, or parakeets. Quite a few families had dogs and cats. I loved them all. In my memory, the cats were invariably Persian and the dogs were either Boston Terriers or Cocker Spaniels. Sadly, the tropical animals and birds rarely made it back to the States with the cats and dogs. Predictably, I started loving "Bambi" when the movie appeared some years later.

I begged for a pet of my own. Though no animal lover, my father indulged me by getting two parakeets, which were to be my sole responsibility. I was to dispense the birdseed and water and clean the cage. Although only nine years old, I did a good job. Yet the beautiful little birds soon died. My father blamed me for their death." You've been assigned a duty," he said, "yet your only response to failure is 'No excuse, sir." Apparently, there was no room in his universe for making allowances, or seeking reasons for slip-ups. That day I learned that for my father, "responsibility" and "blame" were synonyms. Funny, isn't it, how "blame" rhymes with "shame." If something went wrong, the person associated with the mistake was automatically wrong as well.

I was never allowed another pet in the house, and I chose not to risk the responsibility of life or death with any more animal friends until I had become an adult. I was also avoiding any more stern lectures about my shortcomings. I became fearful of my father's disapproval and habitual scoldings for things I could not even comprehend. Whatever understanding I found came from my mother, who could comfort me and help me in my avoidance of my dad's wrath - a wrath she often was subjected to as well.

Blessed with a sunny disposition and a friendly naïveté, I eagerly befriended as many other children my age and their pets as I could. I was also blessed with a stubborn determination. Any loose animal, insect or lizard became my secret charge, along with affection for my friends' pets. In Panama, the study of army ants and anteaters on the ground and iguanas and sloths in the mango trees captured my attention. Many live creatures were subjected to my handling, hugs, and conversation. Tadpoles and frogs caught my interest. To this day, I marvel that as a child I never encountered a poisonous creature, although snakes and scorpions were everywhere I tramped. Apparently, I was destined to have good animal experiences — at least with the small ones.

Big animals were another matter, however, including my muscular father. Before World War II, the Army had cavalry horses and still used mules. My father was a world-class Roman rider, even riding two horses at once, jumping over hurdles. He was also a national champion gymnast. He wanted me to follow his lead. He tried to teach me gymnastics but soon gave up in disgust. I was too supple, too chubby, too weak and too indifferent to please him. Therefore, he enrolled me in horseback riding instead. During the second lesson, I fell off the huge horse and was trampled. Of course, the riding lessons stopped immediately. My name, Philip, means "lover of horses," and indeed I do love them, but I respect them even more and to this day I ride a horse only at a walk.

After the horseback debacle, I believe one final disappointment caused my father to give up on his only child as too much of a sissy, coward, and weak-ling to hold much interest for him. When I was almost ten years old, desperate to "make a man" of me, he paid me the fantastic sum of ten dollars—a fortune in 1939—to pick a fight and not to come home until I was bloodied and had won the fight. I did as he asked, got bloodied and lost—again. Lost the fight and lost the ten dollars.

By then, he was well embarked upon a relation-ship with alcohol that held all his interest. He used my failure to measure up as one among many excuses for drinking, telling me outright that he would rather drink and be with his friends than bother with me. He became hostile, sarcastic, insulting, distant and physically and emotionally unavailable as both a parent and a husband. Whenever I tried to reach out to him, I met only criticism and brutality. His new lover—booze—held far more appeal for him than his weakling son. In the old-time Army, hard drinking was scarcely discouraged. Before I turned twelve I had completely lost my father's companionship, such as it was. My mother had also lost her partner to the disease of alcoholism, along with what was then called manic-depressive illness, now known as bipolar disorder.

In my young mind, my father had turned his back on me in disgust. In turn, I sadly turned away from him and bonded even more closely with my mother. This only made matters worse. His drunkenness and violence became more frightening. On one terrifying occasion, he chased my mother into the bathroom, where she locked the door to protect herself, but then he took a fire ax and chopped down the door to get at her. The terror was overwhelming for both my mother and me. I can still hear the wood splintering and our panic-stricken screams. I had no idea what my mother had to submit to in order to survive that horror but she did. I blacked out this memory until I was 50 years old.

On a fishing trip for tarpon with some of his soldiers, my drunk and reckless father was shooting at turtles and other targets on the shore. Then, uttering obscenities and with a hateful glare, he pointed the pistol at me and started firing it on either side of my terrified face. Two of his soldiers disarmed and restrained him. The boat came to shore, and a kindly sergeant took me on a stroll along the beach out of my father's reach until he could sober up. At that moment, I knew that my father hated me. He never apologized. I wonder today if he even remembered it. Even before that horrifying experience, I never doubted that there was ample reason to avoid this brutal man and every reason to look elsewhere for friendly acceptance and safety.

Consequently, I sought other children and animals to befriend, as well as other father-substitutes whom I could respect and admire. I loved school, the teachers, the other children, the coaches and any sane and sober adult in my life. Naturally, my father regarded these other admired ones in my life as his competitors and enemies out to steal his son – the son that he had already disdained.

Thereafter he became even more cruel and menacing both to my mother and to me. Escape?

When you are living thousands of miles away from any extended family, and the tormentor controls all the money, how can a wife and child flee? We lived in a trap, a prison camp of fear, anger and pain. In a tit-for-tat reaction, I rejected my father and everything about him, including his career. He in turn rejected and resented his child and his wife. Now I began to hate the Army. Tragically, pain and alienation shadowed our little family for the rest of my childhood and beyond.

We accompanied my father after he received orders to return to the States, just before Pearl Harbor. In three years more, although by then he had risen to the rank of lieutenant colonel; continual drinking and outrageous misbehavior finally brought him disgrace and forced medical retirement. With World War II in full swing, the infamy we had felt before was nothing to the extreme shame that now enveloped our lives. My father ran. He fled to Mexico, deserting us, living with prostitutes and squandering all his separation pay. We were sure - and hoped - he would never return.

Living at that time in Austin, Texas, Mother and I knew the bitter taste of poverty. In bitter humiliation, I went house to house begging for food. Our landlord, Arthur Rhodes, saw our plight and soon was providing meals for us as well frequently inviting us to dinner. I took on an enormous paper route. A personal victory at this time was winning the paperboys' contest for a huge Thanksgiving turkey, which fed the two of us for weeks. War shortages and rationing were in full force. We had no car. My father was a failure, a coward and a drunk. I took on his dishonor and disgrace as my own, but it tore me apart to feel such discomfiture surrounded by many military heroes and other kids whose fathers were serving honorably and well.

To salvage some honor out of dishonor, I began to lie, inventing enormous fictions of my father's secret missions, serving the country and the President. All the while, deep within me, hatred was permeating and poisoning my soul. My uncle, my mother's older brother, came to our financial rescue, and we were able to hang on, but I had changed. Though I no longer had to beg, I was depressed, ashamed, anxious and enraged all at the same time. My mother tried valiantly to keep my sagging spirits up, to no avail.

Every one of us has a cruel streak, sometimes well concealed. Now my own cruel streak emerged. The animals I once loved became my victims. I joined up with a neighbor boy in Austin maliciously shooting as many sparrows we could. With our Daisy BB rifles, we shot at any small bird we could find. It no longer occurred to me that I was breaking my promise to never have any life-and-death responsibilities over animals. I had forgotten my two little parakeets. I had also forgotten the saying I had learned in Sunday school about God knowing every sparrow that fell to the ground.

My sparrow-killing rampages went on until I killed a defenseless owl. As his magnificent body lay before me and I spread out his wings, I began to cry. All the pain and anger I had been carrying inside, directed at an absent failure of a father, came gushing out in a cleansing torrent of remorseful tears. I vowed never again to take my rage out on living beings.

Even at this time, I did not realize that my poisonous feelings for my father had been spilling out on the wrong targets. I gave my BB gun away, yet I knew no peace. Almost every night, in the large estate behind our little cottage, I could hear the calls and the hoots of owls –a relentless reminder of the wrong I had done. I stopped hunting at that time, but the cease-fire was not to be a permanent one.

My father returned. He begged Mother for forgiveness and promised never to touch alcohol again—the first of hundreds of such promises to reform that he would never keep. He brought me a puppy, which I deliberately rejected and ignored. He even named it "Mr. Ducrow" a West Point term for lowly first year cadets. That was too close to home to my own lowly status as his son. Moreover, the puppy was his, not mine. Angrily, he gave the puppy away. Things were desperate. We had no money.

We traveled to my great-aunt Ila's home in Columbia, South Carolina, where she also came to our rescue, feeding and housing us while my dad looked for work. He managed to find a position at a Georgia military school, but, predictably, he lost that job within a year. Fortunately, I was able to stay on at the school. My mother went to work at Rich's Department Store in Atlanta. I worked afternoons and summers to finish prep school and won a scholarship and work-study grant that took me through college.

Angels

My years at Georgia Military Academy were blessed years, full of angelic beings. The teachers were angels who reached out to me. The other boys were like angels as well. Naturally, many were roguish angels, but to me, all were like a wonderful new family of brothers. The school itself was like my old heaven, the familiar forts of my early years that had brought me so much peace and joy. The school even greeted each dawn and dusk with bugle calls and a flag ceremony. I had come home. I was restored to paradise.

A famous swim-coach angel came to our school. With his help and nurture, I achieved All-American honors. I found my best-friend angel, Bubba Paget, who brought me to Christ. Academically, I was able to surpass my own expectations. I won an honors appointment to West Point and gleefully turned it down when I was offered admission to Yale University.

All the functions of angels are described in the various religions—Jewish, Christian, Islamic, and others. By these accounts, angels are serendipitous beings who announce, guide, protect, encourage, warn, teach, support and love. I cannot count the host of people-angels who saved me from bitterness and brought me God's joy during those four years of formation and reformation. I therefore became a firm believer in angel-people in my life. People of blessing, goodness and grace have always been in my life. So often, we may be tempted to believe that one person's actions and kindnesses cannot make much difference in the world, but I disagree. I am the grateful beneficiary of just such actions and kindnesses.

During these teen years, my special angels had the names of Elisa Parham, my mother; Thomas and Marian Ott, my uncle and aunt; Commander Lacy, my teacher and mentor; Major and Mrs. Paget, surrogate parents; and Les Fouts, my swimming coach. Other angels' names escape me, but there were many who also blessed me on my way in the midst of trials and travails, surrounded me, and would not let me despair or give up on life or myself. I thank God for the loving care of all these who made the difference for me. I thank them for the courage and inspiration they gave a vulnerable teenager when he needed them most.

My gracious and vivacious mother, still a vital and healthy woman, lived to see me graduate from prep school, go on to succeed in college, get married and rejoice in a first-born daughter. She was my guardian angel of grace and goodness. She gave me a love for life, literature, truth, beauty and God. Without her, I might never have survived. Yet, the burden, the fear and her tragic marriage to my father took its toll. Just before my enrollment in seminary, she suffered a complete emotional and mental breakdown from which she never recovered.

She was spared her any further suffering, however, for she spent the rest of her years unaware of the pain of the past, in a pleasant state of mind in her own world, safely removed and cushioned from harsh reality. I praise God for her and see her sacrifice as

Christlike. She died for me. My mother and all those others who befriended me on my journey taught me to always look for angels, never stop trying, and never be afraid to ask for help. Their persistent love convinced me that God is real and provides angelic help for everyone in human and divine forms. To this day, whenever a need arises—my own or that of someone else—I frequently remember to pray for the support of loving and generous angels to help see the needy one through. They always appear. They always have.

When I began my first year of college, although I gained some satisfaction in rejecting the military and my father's career, I began to be able to recognize some of his paternal blessings even in the midst of curses. In the midst of evil, there is goodness nevertheless. A Sunday school teacher told me, "When you are faced with EVIL, Christ will turn it around to help you LIVE." Even in apparent disasters, I found a measure of redemption.

My father's pathos and pain were a case in point. He was a <u>fallen</u> angel. Yet, all angels do God's bidding. It was God's will and intention that I was led to a garden of life where I could bloom. God led me back to a real fort—a reconstruction of my childhood paradise. Without my father's choices, even his bad ones, I would have never found the blessings of those special years and special places. Furthermore, my father's example of pride in his own championship gymnastic and other athletic achievements resurfaced in me as I became able to feel pride in my own swimming feats.

During my teen years, I rarely saw my father. I went to school early and came home late. Moreover, he was gone for long spells in Army and Veterans Administration hospitals. My bitter feelings of pain and anger toward him turned to melancholy. I no longer found satisfaction in hating him, because I had discovered what a waste of time and energy that was. Someone remarked that hating another person is like swallowing poison yourself, then waiting for the other person to die. I told myself it was better to be sad than mad. Compassion, pity and a deep sadness for his tragic life soon became my habitual feelings. To me, he was a sick, blind guide who had unwittingly maneuvered his son into a full and gracious life. Whatever plan God had for my father, I am grateful, because in living with him I learned so much about *what not to do and how not to be.*

I later realized that when he was his sober and healthy self, my father had also bestowed on me many valuable personal treasures, treasures I was able to claim before he died. He used to be so honorable, true, generous, caring and friendly yet that early self gave way to his illnesses and changed his personality. I prefer to think of him in his former healthy life before he began his path of destruction.

Strangely, I cannot remember a single animal in those eight years of high school and college except for Handsome Dan, the Yale Bulldog. I suppose I could not bear the guilt of animal contact, knowing I had been a bird killer, beginning with my parakeets. I probably simply avoided even looking at all animals, domestic or wild. That majestic owl always seemed to be there looking at me and asking, "Why?" He did not need to ask "Who?" He knew. I knew. I carried this guilt into my adult life.

During the decade between the ages of 13 and 23, I am sure I repressed the guilt that lingered within me about birds. When Ruth and I moved to Phoenix, Arizona, with our year-old daughter, I took up hunting birds again. This time I found another hunting partner, Gordon Cook, and we shot quail and white-winged doves. I was taught the discriminations bird hunters make between game birds and sparrows, hawks, and owls. Sparrows could be shot with impunity, for they were pests. However, one should never kill hawks, owls, eagles or falcons, because they killed rodents and other pests as well as helping to cull the game birds, countering overpopulation and consequent depletion through disease. We bird hunters and avian predators were allies.

With these comforting rationalizations, I continued to hunt birds and later, at my first church assignment in Texas, began hunting deer as well. There most of the congregation hunted and fished for food. Soon after our arrival, our freezer was stocked with donated wild game and other food in a Southern tradition called pounding—church members brought pounds of various kinds of food to welcome us. When that initial store of food diminished, I bought a rifle on credit and hunted my own venison, dove and quail, and learned to fish for food as well. Satisfied that I never sought game trophies or killed for sport, I felt no pangs of guilt or remorse, for by then our family numbered five, and my hunting kept us fed until the spring.

After moving to San Antonio to take up a new church assignment, I continued to hunt for meat with no qualms, until a fellow hunter mistakenly killed a fawn. Then the old owl guilt and heartache returned. I put my guns away into their case. The weight of responsibility for life and death returned. I could find no more need to be a hunter. We had enough money for food. That excuse evaporated. My hunting friends were puzzled. In the end, I gave my guns away.

Matters became worse, when I read a story of a little girl's futile attempt to save stranded starfish by returning them from the beach to the ocean. When asked what difference placing a few such creatures back into the water made, holding a starfish in her hands, she said, "It makes a difference to this one." That sank in. Even one life spared makes a difference. It made a difference to me when I shot that owl—just one owl. I had wantonly killed one of God's creatures.

The Blessings of Pain

Most likely, in my painful experiences with and without my father, I inadvertently learned some of the blessings of pain. Another word for one kind of pain is "tenderness," a word often used by doctors when they look for places "tender to the touch." Fortunately for me, a sensitive tenderness grew up in me, instead of defensiveness or reactive hostility.

Somehow, I learned to trust in God and my mother, yielding my own ego. This is how I have learned the spirituality of pain, and the gift of surrender to God and other helpers. All the twinges, aches and hurtful episodes never seemed to harm or wound me to such an extent that I stopped hoping or looking ahead. Pain did not damage me permanently. It made me sore but not sour. It gave me sensitivity to my self and others, as well as helping me begin to grow into a caring person, rather than a numb or callous one. This I count as a miracle. I was taught how to love. I continue to experience redemptive pain as compassion and sensitivity.

Throughout my life, God has taught me to trust in the midst of fear and pain, to strive and stay alive, to take responsibility and be accountable. I have also been blessed by being taught to be grateful for providence; to never lose heart for God can redeem any situation. I learned to move on, have hope, keep loving and learning and cling to Jesus, my Savior and Lord. I knew that God would send angels. Why not? They have come to me before. My life echoes John Bunyan's words: "Afflictions make the heart more deep, more experimental, more knowing and profound, and so, more able to hold, to contain, and beat more." Early on, I took comfort in St. Paul's words: *"No testing has overtaken you that is not common to everyone. God is faithful, and He will not let you be tested beyond your strength, but with the testing will also provide the way out so that you may be able to endure it." (I Corinthians 10:13.2)*

Although I trusted God's future escape plan and knew that I should count on divine grace, I still felt empty, tired, and unforgiven in spite of God's providence. I understand now that pain tires people out. I was certainly exhausted by the effort to survive. Yet, I was puzzled. Where was my empty feeling coming from? Why this lingering depression? Was I not praying enough? Had I not learned the ways of the spirit? Should I seek more meditative moments and quiet private times with God? Was this part of my guilt? What good was the love I carried in my heart? These questions remained unanswered for years.

Questions to ponder:

1. Have there been times in your life when you felt that your pain was more than you could bear? What were those times? Did God help? Did you ask?
2. Were you able to reach out in need to a loving person—animal or human—in your distress, and did that other person help you receive their love? Name them to God in prayer.
3. If you are still carrying pain about events from the past, might there be someone you love that you could speak to about it now? If you do not know of anybody, might you be willing to pray that you would find such a caring helper? Make an appointment with a pastor.
4. Can you think of times when you may have been an "angel," showing love and care to someone else? How many times have you been thanked when you discounted it? You may have given angelic help in spite of yourself.
5. Has any painful experience in your life caused you to make a complete turnabout in some respect? Have you become tender and more loving? If so, do you recognize this and are you grateful for the change? Will you praise and thank God in Christ and keep it up?

CHAPTER FOUR

From Shame to Spirituality

—ɯ—

The gospel story of the prodigal son and his pouting elder brother display good examples of disabilities. These are disabilities of the spiritual kind, all stemming from extremism, of being out of control, hammer all the way down, foot to the floorboard...in one way or another. A spiritual disability is usually characterized by going overboard. We can go over the line and fall. We can push the envelope to the edge and crash. We do this by thinking, feeling, acting, and being too much. Too much of a good thing is still too much. Both sons fell over board into excess. Both sons in the story are the human race. You and Me.

Take the younger son, the one called "prodigal." Other words for prodigal are: *degenerate, profligate, wasteful, excessive and squanderer, extravagant, immoderate* and *unrestrained*. That describes the younger son all right. Jesus surrounded himself with such sinners. The younger son could have easily have also been the breast-beating publican in the temple who cried, "mercy." Nevertheless, his shame led him to spirituality, to his father's love and grace.

His primary spiritual disability was that he maxed himself out...burned the candle way down, and went way beyond his natural, God-given good qualities. These would include spontaneity, a joy for life, playfulness, good humor and a delight in being "of good cheer." Most of the time, these qualities can be compellingly attractive and invite our participation or admiration. These virtues lighten our loads and light up our life. The disability happens when excessiveness takes over. In the younger son, his excess was wastefulness, immorality, and degenerate and degrading behavior. Too much fun and games become destructive and create "prodigal conduct" to the shameful utmost. Baby brother reached the pits, a victim of his own run-a-way excesses, just like poor Pinocchio.

What is this young man's need in addition to the grace of forgiveness and reunion with his father? Don't you think he could use some of the better qualities of his brother? Like responsibility, self-discipline, hard work and reliability? Maybe he could teach his younger sibling the meaning of duty and devotion to his father. Big brother represented the pinnacle of righteousness.

Let us take the older brother then. He could have been the righteous Pharisee in the temple just like many Jesus knew first hand. Holy Ones. Special Ones. Perfect Ones. Law Abiding Citizens. It is, indeed, a virtue to take one's responsibilities seriously and be one who could be depended upon to do a good job. A strong sense of duty and to have a good moral sense of right and wrong. Nothing is wrong being hard-working, conscientious, reliable, and religious. No vices here. Yet this shamelessness led to his spiritual death and isolation.

The danger of disability in Mr. Reliable is crossing the line into lovelessness, joylessness, self-righteous-ness, judgmentalism, and being imprisoned by duty to such an extent, that forgiveness is forgotten. Law becomes all and Grace evaporates. Impatience and resentment has the self-righteous under their power. Perfectionists practice infinite forms of condemna-tion for those less obedient and dependable. No room in their world for *goofing up* and the *klutzy* among us had better stay clear. Being around such strict, shameless and straight-laced persons is dangerous. They can be downright nasty.

What can redeem such arrogance and grandi-osity? It seems to me that redemption for the Super Son, and every Hero among us, is a heavy dose of the better qualities of the younger Rebel, the Wayward One... If spoons-full of sugar make the medicine go down, then massive spoonfuls of learning to lighten up, letting go, even if it feels foolish and childish. *Serious Sam needs Playful Pete*, and Straight-laced Samantha needs Merry Marilyn to celebrate life not grieve it. Some of us are born to be in perpetual grief with occasional joy, and some are born to be in perpetual joy with occasional grief. Wouldn't you rather see the rose before the thorns?

So, we can fall into both excesses and extremes. Both sons were disabled in spirit. Both sons sinned. So have we. Only the younger one managed miraculously to hear and see reality and as Jesus says, *"come to his senses."* Only this lost sheep took stock of himself, saw himself in the midst of filth and despair, how far he had sunk, faced reality and repented. He looked into the mirror of his extremism. Wouldn't have been grand and gracious if his elder brother took a look at himself as well? Perhaps he did. That is another story.

The older son, sad to say, stays stuck; he becomes even more self-righteous and loveless than ever. Why? Why does he resent his own brother so much? Why did he ask for a party all those years? Why didn't he sing and dance all around the estate and in the aisles before? Why is he so full of bitterness and void of cheer? Why was he such a drag? Such a spoilsport?

It's still a mystery to me, yet a familiar one. Grudges, vengeful spirits, hostility, chips on shoulders, bitter folks are well known to me, but terribly misunderstood. Nothing in my life, as bad as some of it has been, managed to sour me on life. I just don't get it. I see it but cannot fathom it. Someone said "God hides things by putting them before our eyes." Perhaps the elder one was just as blind, as blind to joy as his brother was to righteousness. Yet, what a tragedy, as loved as he was, the elder brother was not content with all his father's treasure and grace. He even felt like a slave, in the midst of paradise in the arms of the kingdom of love and blessing.

Doesn't the father's house represent the Kingdom of heaven? We are the ones who misuse it right under our noses, like the prodigal in us who overused it and consumed all its pleasures and the elder son in us who underused and didn't even know he was already in heaven. He even saw himself as a galley slave, when he was actually the Heir and Prince of the Kingdom. Maybe something like that happened to Lucifer, the prince of angels and of light. He was in the lap of love and goodness and despised it.

Yet the same spirit that picked up the prodigal, was in the bitter brother even if he could not see it. I trust and want to believe that Jesus had another story to tell of the elder's redemption from his disability of rage and hard-heartedness. My prayer is for compassion for this outraged and disappointed fellow and all his descendants. I want so for Mr. Uptight and all his ilk to come into the light and joy of his brother's return, to accept and participate in the father's love and reconcile to his brother and any other losers in his life. Don't you just want to shake him? To find a way to help him give up his pouting and join in the festivities.

You know, I think there is such a story. It is the story of Saul of Tarsus, the avenging and hate-consumed prosecutor and persecutor of the early disciples, who by God's grace was knocked off his high horse, cast into darkness and humbled, humiliated and then lifted up as Paul the Apostle of love, joy, sacrificial obedience, reliable faith and heavenly hope, who received all the gifts of the spirit. I would like to think he was the elder brother, who came home too. So, there is hope for us, who are frozen stiff with icy judgment against others. We too can be thawed out, melted and molded into Christ's own loving disciples. Christ alone is the miracle maker, the softener of our pride and our hard hearts. We can never make that happen alone. May he gives us all soft hearts for prodigals and perfectionists alike and cause us to love *anyone*, even those with the most disgusting and ugly disabilities.

Carol's Control

Carol was a perfectionist who suppressed her prodigal, a "straight-laced Samantha" who hid her "merry Mary." My experiences with managing animals paralleled Carol's journey with management. An intense young woman, she had habitually striven to rule and regulate her own life along with the lives of everyone around her. Well organized, forceful and charming, she managed to get away with her managerial ways because she was also so nurturing, so attentive and helpful to all. Her favorite phrase was, "Here, let me help you do that." A consummate caretaker, she took over and took care of just about everything in sight. She became a dynamite executive, working her way up from the secretarial pool. She was so good at details that nothing escaped her attention and finally her diligent supervision.

On the other hand, no one had a chance to work *with* her, since she did it all. Carol made no room for teamwork. Left alone, she could handle every detail. With others around, she directed their work as well.

Around her, there was no way to contribute any independent ideas or show any personal incentives. It was much easier to let her sweetly take charge. This was a neat deal for some, yet for the majority, who considered themselves grown-up adults, playing little chicks to the mother hen was just too much surrender.

Then things began to change for Carol. Once charming and cheerful, she became easily irritated and reactive. Mother Hen suddenly changed into a Wet Hen, furious with her chicks. No one seemed to cooperate as they once had. "What's wrong with everyone?" she wondered. In her overachieving bravado, she was certain she should and could handle her job, parent her children, keep her home immaculate, organize her family's social life, care for her husband, and run everything and everyone with a smile on her face.

In reality, Carol was out of control as she tried to manipulate herself and others. An underground resistance movement had grown in opposition to her mother-hen behavior. She was used to riding herd over small creatures—as I had in my first blessing of the animals. She had no idea that such creatures could grow into threatening monsters.

Once she had docile and obedient people in her life. Now everyone seemed surly and rebellious. "How can they be so ungrateful and difficult," she complained, "after all I have done for them?" Carol was sincerely surprised by the guerilla warfare that soon surrounded her. Completely puzzled by disobedient children, uncooperative employees, an unavailable husband, distancing friends, and a hostile world, she become terribly depressed. Nothing was going right.

Sadly, she could trust no one else to improve things. She kept on doing what she had been doing and expecting different results, without realizing that such thinking and behavior is one definition of insanity. This tactic had always worked before. Accustomed to forcing solutions, she knew no other way. She soldiered on, rolling up her sleeves to battle the beasts with redoubled efforts. Yet she found out some problems are just too big, bigger even than a bunch of wild horses. Horses do not push around easily, even with Carol. The thought that she could have allowed her wild horses to run free never occurred to her. How sad that she missed the joy of witnessing beautiful horses galloping freely through a field. She once shared that she always supervised her children's play and never tolerated "horse play."

As her challenges piled up into gigantic unattended stacks of work, as days no longer had enough hours, and as she experienced herself all alone and friendless, Carol did try something that was different and unusual. She looked around for help and even hinted for some assistance. Without realizing how her own internal state had shifted to another controlling stance, she switched from mother to martyr. She left off nurturing-control in favor of criticizing-control, two sides of the same coin.

Resorting to self-pity, complaining, and nagging, she tried to use guilt and shame to force conformity. Sarcasm, tears, and accusations became her sincere and desperate attempts to gain submissiveness and reassert her dominance. She unconsciously decided that if nice will not work, maybe nasty will get results.

Sovereignty was her goal. Regardless of whether this urge comes from a kind and overly nurturing mother or from a harsh and critical one, it is still parental, and that equals control. Furthermore, when any style is employed to gain a victory over others, it amounts to selfish and insensitive coercion. Such constraint disregards choice and shows disrespect for others' capabilities. Sweet or sour, chains are chains.

This compulsion to rule and reign, even covered in parental clothing, is really the same emotional ploy used by three-year-olds to get their way. Sweetness and seduction one minute, and temper tantrums the next, the ego state of the three-year-old can continue to plague grown-ups with the age-old mistake of— acting as if we are the center of our own universe.

Fortunately for her, Carol found no one either willing or able to assist her in her quest for command and the refuge of an egocentric world. Fed up with her ruling and overruling, her chicks became quite unruly. Puzzled and hurt looks met her attempts to assert herself and hold sway. Her influence was wavering. Questioning her sanity and implying possession of some sort, the chicks spitefully rose up against mother hen. Subordinates have an insubordinate way of getting even. What demon did possess her? Was its name really control?

The sad truth was that no one caught in the unhealthy dynamic could unravel this mystery or identify the real culprit. Carol had no insight into her dilemma and neither did anyone else. She thought she was surrounded by ingrates, while the "ingrates" simply reacted to oppression and emotional abuse. A good friend of mine who worked with the have-nots of the world once wisely remarked, "Yesterday's oppressed become tomorrow's oppressors."

Obviously, something like a revolution was going on, and the people Carol attempted to govern were seeking to throw off their chains. This was an accurate description of the situation, yet it was no explanation. Why this was happening was still a mystery.

Never looking to her own behavior or her own contributions to this conflict, Carol was sure it was everyone else's fault. She could not see that she had unwittingly, and with the best of intentions, helped to create this all-encompassing dynamic of ruler and servants, creating the setting for a full-scale rebellion.

If Carol was the mother hen, then her chicks were her associates, co-workers, children, husband, pets, and friends—anyone firmly established in a "less than" role to her "more than" position. Over the years, most of her chicks had gotten used to her over- responsibility, while she had gotten used to their compliant under-responsibility. This over/under responsibility system was well in place and very difficult to change. It had become the norm, the expected structure of life for Carol and Company.

Carol's control system could work either of two ways. Either the chicks would forever be chicks, or mother hen would always be in charge. The chicks would peep in obedient and dependent neediness, and mama would take them under her wings to protect, nurture, and above all, dominate. Or, in the second way, the chicks would run away, resist, rebel, act out, and misbehave, while Mama would then chase, peck, flap her wings, cluck disapprovingly, and likewise go on attempting to control. Chicks will be chicks. Hens will be hens.

Carol forgot that chicks grow up into hens and roosters, and that peers cannot be treated like children. Nor did she acknowledge that there were already a lot of grown-up hens and roosters in the world. Grown-ups do better with grown-ups in an equable, cooperative system of respect and collaboration. At least since the American Revolution, freedom seems to be instinctive for people in this country. Monarchs do not do well in "the land of the free and the home of the brave." Autocrats like Carol invite rebellion.

At this frustration point, it did not occur to Carol that she was living the life of a despot. Yet, she also inhabited a world of denial, even delusion. She really was blind to what everyone else could see—that she was addicted to power, even tyranny. Fortunately, however, she was not far away from admitting that her life was truly unmanageable and out of control, edging closer to feeling helpless and hopeless, leading to the discovery of the real demon in her life.

Surprisingly, her deliverers were her disobedient subjects, who were now intervening to break down her wall of denial and isolation. Her family and other subordinates loved her. They loved her enough to get her into counseling, and some of them also agreed to join in as fellow counselees.

Thank God, there was enough health and good will left among her family and friends that what was "meet and right" broke through, providing relief and redemption for everyone involved. This is a classic case of the oppressed freeing their oppressor as well as themselves, liberating both sides of the impasse. When suffering and misery go on too long, protests emerge. The Protestant revolt from Roman Catholic corruption and tyranny is an historical case in point.

Carol's Capitulation

When Carol and Company came to see me for family therapy, she was still consumed with trying to command everything in her life, only asking for help in regaining her position of authority. To the others, this was not enough. Their goal was to level the playing field and deal themselves into the game. They were tired of fighting and losing, and hoped that Carol was ready to delegate and trust others and even step aside or step down off her throne.

She did admit to feeling frazzled and about to fall apart. Asked by all if she would like to rest for a bit, she looked as if such a blessing would be heaven itself. In love and concern, her former subjects suggested she take a vacation and let go of all responsibilities for a while. That sounded so good to her, she agreed to do so as long as everyone agreed not to "beat up on her" and humiliate her. At this point, I saw that her loved ones had compassion for her fragile emotional state and would not become tomorrow's oppressors. I appreciated and admired this hopeful sign. With guidance and common courtesy, no one would have to be shown up or put down.

If Carol could just abdicate for a spell and vacate her throne room, she might find out how good it can feel not to be responsible for everyone and everything in her life. Carol could then learn how to be responsible – and responsive - to herself and others. She agreed to try. I applauded her bravery. I suggested that perhaps she simply did not understand the over/under responsibility scheme that was running her life. Letting everything slide and trusting others to take charge, even for a while, was scary for her and I sympathized with her. We talked about how simple it could be if she could understand the difference between being responsible for or being responsible to others. With the simple chart below, we discussed the difference.

When I am responsible FOR others, I	When I am responsible TO others, I
Carry feelings.	Encourage and cheerlead
Take over.	Support
Control.	Set the other free
Bear burdens.	Trust the other
Feel Tired and angry.	Feel refreshed and proud
Fix things.	Do not fix
Manage	Help when asked
Disrespect	Respect.
Am a Manipulator	Am a friend

Working with the family to find ways to use the responsibility chart with real situations at home, within weeks we made progress in liberating each person. We also examined together the four steps of the learning and counseling process: *reveal, feel, deal,* and *heal.*

First, Carol *revealed* her history, going back over all the family dynamics that had been influential in her life. From doing that, we discovered that her hidden problem was "shamefulness," a deep *feeling* of inadequacy. Apparently, this was not ordinary embarrassment or bashfulness. Humbleness is an unpretentious and admirable admission of our fallible humanity, which is (in my opinion) healthy and a source of spirituality. Jesus declared his blessings on such meekness in the Beatitudes. (Matthew 5:5)

Humility and Humiliation

Meekness is the doorway to humility, the opposite of arrogance and pride. Yet, Carol was the victim of a sort of unworthiness that was filled to the core with insufficiency and worthlessness. This was once called by Calvin "total depravity," and by Anglicans "miserable sinners" and by Roman Catholics "scrupulosity." None of these is honest, accurate or healthy.

Her worthless feeling was traced back to her negative and critically controlling mother, who was impossible to please. Carol *dealt* with this dilemma by vowing never to be like her mom, choosing to take control of herself as she set out to prove her worth and show her mother. What she thought she had to demonstrate to her mother was that she was good, worthy, valuable, cherished and acceptable – everything she was missing from her mother's lack of affirmation. When one feels useless, trying to be useful makes sense. When we feel hollow and insignificant it is understandable to fill ourselves up with significance and bolster our importance.

She believed, mistakenly, that powerful efforts to control everything and everybody would make up for her deeply ingrained feeling of worthlessness or shamefulness. She would do this by becoming the most positive and nurturing person she could be - and thereby find *healing*. We both agreed that her vow had been a worthy one, but she had inadvertently put her mother in charge of her life and had unconsciously done the unthinkable – wound up acting just like her.

I asked, "Why not really free yourself and your mother as well this time, by making good on your promise and being and acting like yourself rather than a negative or positive copy of your mom?" She agreed that she was tired of being the boss and fighting so hard to prove her worth to mother and everyone else. Certainly, that was what her family was hoping for.

Sharing with her how little control Jesus exerted over others, his power was the power of attraction and not force or manipulation. He held out an invitation not a weapon. When his followers saw someone doing good works and healing without using Jesus' name, he told his disciples to "let them be." If they are doing good, that is to everyone's benefit even if they do not seem to have the right credentials.

How different we often are! We try to get people to do it our way, or to follow our rules. Forcing others into our mold just does not work. Applauding and accepting others' good results and appreciating the distinct differences in people is much more productive. Letting someone truly "do their own thing" is a blessed gift of respect.

It is so easy to give advice and try to shape others into our own ideas and behaviors. We are all guilty of manipulating others, even though we hate it when we are manipulated. Carol knew first hand how hard such maneuvering is, yet understandable when we realized how valiantly she was trying to cover her disrepute.

So together as family and therapist, we discovered that a crushing sense of inadequacy was her real demon, one that was beginning to possess the children's sense of worth as well. I suggested that uncovering this demon could really become her salvation and her family's too. If she could admit her imperfection, her human fallibility and her honest insufficiency and stop trying cover it up by pretending perfection in herself and demanding perfection in others, there was hope.

If she could admit that her life was unmanageable and out of control, then she could move on to the place where hope and help were to be found. There she could find healthy meekness, modesty and true humility and the gift of spirituality – shame-redeemed. The alternative was to keep on living in insolent *shamelessness* as an offending controller or in futile *shamefulness* suffering humiliation and worthlessness. With insight and practice she could learn the blessings of a healthy balance in her relationships and accept her own and others' honest and humble humanity.

Christ does not ask those of us who are trying to recover from our compulsions to wallow in our remorse. How can we reach out for help if we feel no need for healing and forgiveness? "To have no shame" can mean we become numb to the twinges of conscience within us and become shameless. Jesus does not blame and condemn our shortcomings. However, he does want us to see and admit our character defects. Why? So, they can be removed, of course. Our Lord wants us to feel our inadequacy only long enough to get rid of it. However, we need to feel the burden before we can lay it down.

Some of us, however, imagine guilt where there is none. Guilt says to us, "I made a mistake." Shame says to us, "I am a mistake." Becoming addicted or bald, having asthma or diabetes, not being pretty or rich contain no guilt. The way we were created is not our fault. We are responsible for our actions [guilt] –what we actually did, such as lying, cheating, stealing, hurting others. That is where guilt belongs. Guilt is where accountability and repair belong.

Shame makes a proper fit as the feeling we experience when we know we continually "mess up" and look at ourselves as capable of only making "messes" and feel like a mess. Feeling like trash is extreme shame and attacks our very being, deep inside of the self. We can manage guilt over our deeds by making amends. Only a divine, higher power can heal our inner feelings of shame and worthlessness. Redemption is *shame repair.*

When we can "humbly admit" what we have done, then we can take the humble and cleansing steps that remove the guilt and heal the shame. Humility is an essential part of recovery. Pride is not. Our recovery never neglects to say, "Forgive us our sins as we forgive those who sin against us."

The Jewish Talmud says, "*A sense of shame is a lovely thing in a man. Whoever has a sense of shame will not sin so quickly; but whoever shows no sense of shame in his face, his father surely never stood on Mount Sinai.*" I take this to mean reticence and diffidence in the face of God. It is not "shame" as "shame-fulness," ready for the refuse dump but appropriate humility in the face of divine awesomeness.

Joining the Human Race

I introduced Carol and the family group to the first three cleansing steps of Twelve-Step recovery, which is, briefly, "I can't, God can, let God," in that order. In tears, she cried, "I know I can't! Can God really help?" then answered her own question, "If I let God?" I told her that was my firm belief, and I thought it was worth a try. She cried, "Oh, I want to, I want to so much!"

"That's the first big step," I told her. "You never have to learn how to want. All creatures have desire." I shared with her my new knowledge that in Hebrew the word translated "living soul or being" in Genesis 2:7 is the word "nephesh"—literally, "living appetite." I asked her if she really was hungry for God's help. She nodded. "That's great," I said, "because that is the one requirement for recovery, the desire to stop doing what you have been doing

When we welcome God's healing love, we allow love to flow. We use no force, no struggle, no strain, no competition, no trying harder, and no willpower of our own. We simply give up and give in to God. We admit and accept our weakness and God's strength. When we take this first step of surrender and admit our out-of-control powerlessness, we become open to God's own miracle. We learn how wonderful and blessed it is to receive and accept, to be vulnerable and defenseless before God. We stop declaring our own independence. We become like little children; we abandon our own unmanageable control and allow love to manage and control us. When we let go and let God, we give up our natural compulsion for power, to be right, to be managing directors, and let God manage our lives from now on. Carol decided to try her best to allow God the management of her life.

From that day on, Carol lived more deeply into her true self, her real self; the self God wanted her to be. She is beginning to learn her life lessons. She is on her way to freedom. Her first step has been simply, to relax. With courage and determination, she has declared independence from her old habits and vowed to replace them with healthy ones. Declaration, of course, is one thing; doing it is another.

Yet, it is happening for Carol. With God's help, she has faced her demon of shamefulness and accepted her worth as God's child. She knows that she is a human *being* and a human *becoming* no longer merely a human *doing*. She is making progress in no longer refusing to disrespect herself or anyone else, trying to love, honor, and cherish herself and others as fellow children of God. I cannot think of anything better for any of us.

No more stressful over/under relationships for her now. To the best of her ability, she operates on equal terms with almost everyone. She lives on an adult and peer level instead of the superior parent level. She enjoys being a little child at times and is learning to play. She attacks problems and not persons, seeking solutions with others and with God's help. She listens. She learns. She has stopped showing and telling. She asks, shows interest and curiosity.

Today, she is going weekly to CODA, Codependents Anonymous. Finding herself on a level playing field now, she understands that the ground is not so far to fall down to, compared to the distance from the mountain she was looking down from before. I always receive new insights whenever I reflect on this passage:

> *"Whatever house you enter, first say, 'Peace be to this house!' And if anyone is there who shares in peace, your peace will rest on that person; but if not, it will return to you. "*(Luke 10:5-6)

Although it has taken a long time, I have discovered that the opposite of control is peace. We often say, 'All I want is peace of mind, yet we keep on trying to force solutions and resort to "white knuckle" exertions in order to keep everything and everybody "under control". Maintaining control is not peaceful. Jesus gives us his way - the way of "Letting Be" or "Acceptance."

Our Lord calls us first to accept ourselves, something Carol is striving to accomplish. Jesus encourages each of us to be who we are. He also reminds us that we are to accept the lives of others as well. "Live and Let Live" is a word from the Lord as well as a key slogan of all twelve-step programs. All recovery is a process of being delivered from the clutches of control. Self-control and other-control lie at the heart of our spiritual illnesses.

Jesus tells us that if we offer our peace, we cannot lose! Either our peace will "rest upon a son of peace" or it will return to us. (Luke 10:5) When we freely give, what we volunteer will either "rest or return", without our efforts to control or manipulate the results. Carol has two favorite scriptures:

> *"My grace is sufficient for you, for power is made perfect in weakness."* (2 Corinthians 12: 9)

> *"For mortals it is impossible, but not for God; for God all things are possible."* (Mark 10:27)

Questions to ponder:

1. Are there any situations in my life in which I feel out of control? What are they? Have you asked for wisdom?

2. What is it about these areas that I would like to see changed? Are you trying to manage on your own? Can scripture reveal some new pathways to freedom?

3. Is it possible that I have been following orders from someone else, living or dead, on how I should live my life? Have they become like gods to you?

4. Am I willing to ask God or a pastor what areas they see in which I might grow?

5. Am I willing to offer up my challenges to God, asking for His help in solving them?

CHAPTER FIVE

From Abuse to Friendship

—ᶬᵛ—

First Dog

*I*t has been widely reported by an UNRELIABLE
source that the following addition to the Book of
Genesis was discovered in some ancient scrolls that
said:

And Adam said, "Lord, when I was in the garden,
you walked with me every day. Now I do not see you
any more. I am lonesome here, and it is difficult for
me to remember how much you love me."

And God said, "I will create a companion for
you who will be with you forever and who will be a
reflection of my love for you, so that you will know
how much I love you, even when you cannot see me.
Regardless of how selfish and unlovable you may be
this new companion will accept you as you are and
will love you as I do, in spite of yourself."

And God created a new animal to be a companion
for Adam. And it was a good animal. And God was

pleased. And the new animal was pleased to be with Adam, and he wagged his tail. And Adam said, "Lord, I have already named all the animals in the Kingdom, and all the good names are taken. I cannot think of a new name for this new animal."

And God said, "Because I have created this new animal to be a reflection of my love for you, his name will be a mirror image of my own, and you will call him Dog."

And Dog lived with Adam and was a companion to him and loved him. And God was pleased. And Dog was content and wagged his tail.

During our married life, many wonderful dogs have blessed us. In the beginning of our marital Garden of Eden was Lad, and our most recent companion was Runtsy. Between our first Genesis dog and our most recent dog, more than forty years and almost a dozen dogs have traveled with us. All have been as loved, loving, and lovable as suggested by the unbiblical story above. We have many cherished memories of every one. Our family is solidly in the dog-lover camp, although we love all animals. My appreciation for all our doggie friends echoes this anonymous canine-lover's expression of admiration:

"He is your friend, your partner, your defender and your dog. You are his life, his love and his leader. He will be yours, faithful and true, to the last beat of his heart. You owe it to him to be worthy of such devotion."

Our first dog was a German shepherd. We bought him in El Paso in 1954 at the recommendation of friends, Rich and Jeannie Culpin, who owned the same breed. His A.K.A. name was "Aladdin of Kateri," and he came from the famous Longworth Shepherds of California. We bought little Lad as a three-week old pup when my wife, Ruth, was pregnant with Susan, our first child, so he was our first "baby." Our love was instant, and I recalled such a love expressed by the author Edith Wharton for her own new puppy: "My little dog – a heartbeat at my feet."

For some time Lad was at our feet, under our feet, under the bed, under the covers, and a constant heartbeat that stole our hearts. Although we bought him to be a guard dog to protect Ruth and our new girl-child from danger when I was away from home on long business trips, he was a great deal more than that.

I had a "guy thing" with this wonderful macho dog. I called him Lad, while Ruth and little Susan called him Laddie, Laddykins, Laddyboy and many other endearing sweet names. To me he was always Lad. He grew into a black behemoth, weighing in close to a hundred pounds and 100% watchdog. Each of our children was welcomed into a world blessed by him. He was our playmate, friend, protector, comforter and child. He was family. To me, Lad was an angelic gift who taught me to love him and to care for him as a "brother" in my brother less life. A blessing sent to love us and visit with us for a while; he was more like an angel, who did indeed become our guardian angel.

All my life I have heard people talk of their pets as both family members and babies. I like that. What

I do not like is hearing dogs described as "nearly like a person," as if somehow the dog lacked a personality and did not deserve the full respect of a human person. Someone has said that to speak of a dog as almost human, is insulting because a dog can do many things humans cannot do, never could do and never will do. I have even heard it said that the average dog is a nicer person than the average person. Sometimes I am bound to agree. I received this clever description from a friend' email:

"If you can start the day without caffeine or pep
    pills,
If you can be cheerful, ignoring aches and pains,
If you can resist complaining and boring people
    with your troubles,
If you can eat the same food everyday and be
    grateful for it,
If you can understand when loved ones are too
    busy to give you time,
If you can overlook when people take things out
    on you when, through no
fault of yours, something goes wrong,
If you can take criticism and blame without
    resentment,
If you can face the world without lies and
    deceit,
If you can conquer tension without medical
    help,
If you can relax without liquor,
If you can sleep without the aid of drugs,
Then you are probably the family dog."

One of dogs' most endearing aspects is that instead of wagging their tongues they wag their tails. In today's television babble and incessant noise, having a dog to talk to is not only peaceful but also actually healing and redemptive. With your dog, you are profound. Christopher Morley said it well: "No one appreciates the very special genius of your conversation as a dog does." Who can listen better and more positively? How easy to become conceited if seen in your dog's eyes?

Lad proudly kept his head and his tail high. Our German Shepherd Club members told us the tail of the Alsatian should flow gently downward to the ground in the classic Shepherd pose. However, we were not looking for a classic show dog, just a good sentinel. As we trained Lad in his obedience classes we found him so eager to work, to please, and to learn that parading him in a show was irrelevant. As far as we were concerned, our high-tailed friend could carry himself any way he chose. As with all dogs, Lad's tail was his emotional signal. Of course, when he wagged it vigorously in the house, bric-a-brac often went flying. Lad was a perfect example of the old saying; "A dog can express more with his tail in minutes than his owner can express with his tongue in hours."

We were truly blessed by this tail waving, happy, energetic, strong, loving and loyal first dog. I miss him. No new dog ever took his place in my heart. He is there still, and I can see him, feel him, hear him and even smell his glossy coat. Whenever I see him in an old movie or video I want to call him, hug him, and play with him again. He still boosts my sagging spirits. The way I feel about my Lad is illumined by this story.

A man and his dog were walking along a road. The man was enjoying the scenery, when it suddenly occurred to him that he was dead. He remembered dying, and that the dog had been dead for years. He wondered where the road was leading them.

After a while, they came to a high, white stone-wall along one side of the road. It looked like fine marble. At the top of a long hill, it was broken by a tall arch that glowed in the sunlight. When he was standing before it, he saw a magnificent gate in the arch that looked like mother of pearl, and the street that led to the gate looked like pure gold. He and the dog walked toward the gate, and as he got closer, he saw a man at a desk to one side. When he was close enough, he called out, "Excuse me, where are we?"

" This is Heaven, sir," the man answered.

" Wow! Would you happen to have some water?" the man asked.

" Of course, sir. Come right in, and I'll have some ice water brought

right up." The man gestured, and the gate began to open.

"Can my friend," gesturing toward his dog, "come in, too?" the traveler asked.

"I'm sorry, sir, but we don't accept pets."

The man thought a moment and then turned back toward back toward the road and continued the way he had been going. After another long walk, and at the top of another long hill, he came to a dirt road, which led through a farm gate that looked as if it had never been closed. There was no fence.

As he approached the gate, he saw a man inside, leaning against a tree and reading a book.

"Excuse me!" he called to the reader. "Do you have any water?"

"Yeah, sure, there's a pump over there" The man pointed to a place that could not be seen from outside the gate. "Come on in."

" How about my friend here?" the traveler gestured to the dog.

" There should be a bowl by the pump."

They went through the gate, and sure enough, there was an old-fashioned hand pump with a bowl beside it. The traveler filled the bowl and took a long drink himself, and then he gave some to the dog.

When they were full, he and the dog walked back toward the man who was standing by the tree waiting for them.

" What do you call this place?" the traveler asked.

" This is Heaven," was the answer.

" Well, that's confusing," the traveler said. "The man down the road said that was Heaven, too."

" Oh, that place? Nope. That's Hell."

" Doesn't it make you mad for them to use your name like that?"

" No. I can see how you might think so, but we're just happy that they screen out the folks who'll leave their best friends behind." (Internet Quote from Steve Caldwell, August 2001)

This wonderful dog was the first creature that gave me a sense of success with pets. From my failure with parakeets, to rejecting a puppy from my father, to shooting sparrows culminating in killing an owl – Lad was my first animal victory and best friend. Encouraged and consoled by this victory I began to want to embrace all animals again, and felt like Walt Whitman in his *"Song of Myself."*

> "I think I could turn and live with the
>   animals
> they are so placid and self-contained.
> I stand and look at them long and long.
> They do not sit and whine about their
>   condition,
> They do not lie awake in the dark and weep
>   for their sins,
> They do not make me sick discussing their
>   duty to God,
> Not one is dissatisfied, not one is demented
>   with the mania of owning things,
> Not one kneels to another, nor to his kind
>   that live thousands of years ago,
> Not one is respectable or unhappy over the
>   whole earth."

Lad provided more than an ordinary dog. He was my angel and still influences my life for the better. He became my totem or sacramental presence. He became my strength and my support. During the eight years of his life, Lad served as my Barnabas (Son of Encouragement) especially with my Dad. Lad was an antidote to Dad. His obvious nobility and strength flowed into me. I thought that my father would retire into the background after our marriage. I must have been deluded. His abuse and brutal ways continued and his poison spread into our little family.

Whenever my father visited and started acting out and displayed his mean streak, Lad gave me courage to withstand these onslaughts. This was a mysterious spiritual strengthening that came from an animal, somehow inspiring his master to be a man. Lad became a symbol of courage to me. He was more than a badge of my manhood, he was sacramental, in the same way, and I imagine that animal totems somehow imbue Native American consciousness with admired animal characteristics. Lad and I became closely identified. He was my symbolic metaphor for masculinity.

This mystical identity became the hallmark of my own bravery. He made me bold in the presence of my father. I looked to my magnificent German shepherd as my alter ego. He became my staff of Moses. Lad gave me guts and bravado around a father who still could make me feel four years old when I was forty, whenever I was alone with him.

Lad started out with us in El Paso, Texas, moved on with us to Phoenix, Arizona, and then back to Texas again — Dallas, then Austin, then Pleasanton. He was with us for almost nine years, dying in the church rectory. Grateful for all Lad's years with us, all five of us grieved over the loss of our dear friend and my strong support.

Many significant events took place on Lad's watch. Our second child, Sharon, was born in Dallas. God called me to enter seminary in Austin where our third child, Sandy, was born. In the second year of my first church assignment at All Saints Episcopal Church in Pleasanton Lad died. He had been there for the birth of three beautiful daughters and journeyed with us through the most intense times of our lives. Those were good times, special formative times for all of us. We were all like pilgrims on a journey, and we shall always thank God for Lad and his life with us during those vital years. My mourning over Lad and missing him, even today, has helped to deepen my sensitivity to loss and grief in others and helped me understand my own pilgrim's progress.

In contrast to us, with our canine fellow traveler, poor Christian in John Bunyan's classic allegory *Pilgrim's Progress* was on a solitary journey, in which he encountered many trials, temptations, setbacks, and personifications of the spiritual life paths. He seemed to battle his challenges alone most of the time. Luckily for me my wife and daughters, grandchildren, and friends, our dogs have all been in the caravan. We found trouble. Trouble found us, but in the process we found each other's friendship. We often joked that we were like Gypsies. My chief blessing has been to be part of a close, loving family — all the more so because I am an only child.

Ron Thomson, a very close friend and another only son, is also a pet-lover supreme. Both Ron and his wife, Doris, find themselves today in the same pet circumstances as Ruth and I, dog lovers without our own dogs. Nevertheless, we love everyone else's pets. It is a bit like being grandparents. You can indulge them, love them, and then turn them back over to the parents. I rejoice and give thanks to God for the Thomsons, who have been with us through cancer, suffering, and disappointments and are always there to keep on loving us. They are powerful proof s of God's love and presence in our world.

It is amazing how little control Jesus exerted over others. His power was the power of attraction and not force or manipulation. He held out an invitation not a weapon. When his followers saw someone doing good works and healing without using Jesus' name, he told his disciples to "let them be". If they are doing good, that is to everyone's benefit even if they don't seem to have the right credentials.

How different we often are! We try to get people to do it our way, or to follow our rules. Forcing others into our mold just does not work. Applauding and accepting others' good results and appreciating the distinct differences in people is much more productive.

When was the last time you truly let someone "do their own thing"? It is so easy to give advice and try to shape others into our own idea of Christianity. Is your friend showing the gifts of the Holy Spirit...joy, peace, courage, kindness, love? Are they more open, secure and considerate? Do they listen? Are they growing in confidence and enthusiasm for the God of their understanding? Are they doing good works of health and healing and help in Christ's name? Well that's what matters! They are with us, not against us.

Jesus also told us also that *"The kingdom of God is not just coming with signs to be observed; for behold, the kingdom of God is within you."* (Luke 17:20-21) and having this kingdom within means that we don't always have it all figured out and can expect God to be working in many unusual circumstances, by unusual people, and in unusual ways.

In other words, letting God be God. Part of "Letting Go and Letting God" is not only surrendering to His will but also being open to his unexpected action. God has a way all His own that frequently surprises us. Just when we become comfortable with His regular ways, he does something quite irregular.

A story from the Jewish tradition tells of a man lost in a jungle. He tried frantically to find his way, but remained hopelessly lost. Suddenly, he was filled with terror. He saw in the distance what seemed to be a wild beast coming toward him. He could not run. He was frozen with fear. As the beast came closer, he was filled with relief. It looked like a domesticated animal. As the beast came closer, he could see it was a man on a horse. Stirring up all his courage, he moved forward to meet the man. When he reached up to shake the man's hand...he looked into the eyes of his own brother! What a relief!

Although this life contains many beasts of prey, most of them of the human kind, we can meet our own brothers and sisters if we live through fear. Many friends appear to be enemies, even ferocious animals at a great distance, yet as distance is removed...as we grow closer and extend our hand of friendship we may find our own family.

We experience such closeness in our church. Yet, even within such a loving group there will be fear, mistrust and distance. When we look outside our groups to other churches, temples, civic clubs, the neighborhood, we often find the same elements. When we begin to realize that we are all human, with the same fears, hopes and dreams, perhaps we will move through our suspicion and fear and reach out to others in love.

It is in love that we find fear's antidote because *"there is no fear in love, but perfect love casts out fear"* (1 John 4:18). Jesus is perfect love. In his name and spirit and with his presence in us, we too, can learn to love more and fear less. More love equals less fear. Less fear creates more love. How can we lose with that equation?

May our prayer be, *"Christ help us to be fearless, and to be full of love. Create more trust in us, and let us see our brothers and sisters in more places as I move closer to everyone."*

It is risky to trust God. Yet, our risk is our triumph. Every victory begins with risk. Winners also lose at times, but they "keep on keeping on," risking failure each time. Nevertheless, each time adds up to winning, and even the failures turn to victories. No matter how yesterday went, success is for today, and to love is to succeed. Christ wants our success...and with Him, we will win with him.

As I move forward through life now, looking back, I understand the journey more fully by comparing it to the four states of spiritual growth identified by St. Bernard of Clairvaux. I have used Bernard's four names but have filled in each title with my own understandings, which I hope are not counter to his. Naturally, I hope that the noble and heroic St. Bernard dog was named for this saint from Clairvaux. Here is how I see the spiritual journey now.

Modes of Spiritual Growth
With acknowledgements to Bernard of Clairvaux.

In this discussion, "mode" means aspect, state, or condition, and though the modes are commonly taken in order from I to IV, we can slip and slide back and forth, depending on many factors. There is always the danger when numbering such things that we can be guilty of "pigeonholing" and seem mechanistic. Nevertheless these spiritual states have been observed by modern scholars and educators – for example, James W. Fowler in his *Stages of Faith* (New York: Harper & Row 1981), John H. Westerhoff in his *Will Our Children have Faith?* (New York: Morehouse 2000,), and Ronald Goldman in his *Readiness for Religion* (Harper San Francisco 1980), who all see a modal development in stages, progressing from infancy to adulthood. Their research is helpful and enlightening, but for me nothing describes what I have experienced better than St. Bernard of Clairvaux from the fourteen century.

Recently some physicians and therapists have been calling medical procedures, modalities, coming from "model," I suspect. Something like modality is what I mean. Theses are models or approaches of thought, feeling and belief. We can experience all four ways in our lives. God certainly allows that, and knows we cannot be always be in Mode III or Mode IV. Nor does he expect us to be, accepting us wherever we are in our journey.

There is no doubt that I experienced the first two modes of St. Bernard most often as I tried to deal with the torment of my father. The last two states came more frequently into my life as he aged, when he could do no physical harm, and I was free to have more friendship, compassion and pity instead of fear and anger.

Mode I: Love of Self for Self's Sake

This is the manner, or spiritual condition, of utter dependency, complete neediness, self-desire. Here we are immersed in narcissism and self-absorption. This is described by Dr. Harry Tiebout as "his majesty, the baby" in which we are the center of our own universe. This state of spirituality is like walking inside a hall of mirrors. Our own image is reflected everywhere. We see the self in all directions, and our focus may be summed up this way: "I am the Lord my God, and I shall have no other gods before me." John Tillotson of the 17th century said apropos of this mode:

"Men expect that religion should cost them no pains, that happiness should drop into their laps without any design and endeavor on their part, and that, after they have done what they please while they live, God should snatch them up to heaven when they die. But though 'the commandments of God be not grievous', yet it is fit to let men know that they are not thus easy." C. S. Lewis said, "We get out of life that which we love the most and we may get our self alone."

The danger in remaining in Mode I: Solitary confinement for all eternity.

Mode II: Love of God for Self's Sake

This is an improvement over the egocentric self, but the ego is still first. God, in this understanding of the development of the soul, is a <u>means,</u> and the self is still the <u>end</u>. Here we have God "going my way," on board for our agendas.

At this point or place, prayers of <u>petition</u> and <u>confession</u> are our prayers of choice, full of "Help me," "Give me," and "Forgive me." God is servant, and we are still masters and mistresses. At worst, we are our own gods and goddesses. The only answer to prayer we want here is "Yes," and if we do not get that answer, we believe our prayers are not answered at all. We do not see, at this point in our pilgrimage, that a "No" answer may be a "Yes" in disguise, a "Yes" beyond our limits of sight or understanding. Many Christians are at this juncture, still straining to meet selfish goals.

Here, although our motivation is to be with God, it is still for self's sake alone. This is the period of life in which many serious and uptight Christians get stuck. Earnest Christians often miss God by overshooting, oversteering, overstraining, and over controlling. Too many of us live in this stressful world desiring heaven, goodness, joy, and all the spiritual gifts, but for the self first and foremost. Is the only thing you want to be saved? Rescued from Hell? Gain Eternal Life? Then this state is for you. If you get what you want, why go farther, deeper, or higher?

To this phase Henry Van Dyke spoke well:

> "Who seeks for heaven alone to save his
> soul,
> May keep the path, but will not reach the
> goal;
> While he who walks in love may wander far,
> But God will bring him where the Blessed
> are."

The danger in remaining in Mode II: Fanatical self-seeking with God on my side.

Mode III: Love of God for God's Sake

When we find ourselves in this state of being, we discover God as God. Abraham Lincoln said that he was not so much worried about having God on his side as he was about being on God's side. In this chapter, we come to know exactly what Lincoln was talking about. We are ready to let God be God. We love God as God. Now God is both means and end. Prayers of <u>adoration</u>, <u>praise</u>, thanksgiving, and <u>self-offering</u>. All proceed from being in love with God, and for no other reason. The pilgrim in this period responds like a child on a loving parent's lap, who, when asked by the parent why the lap sitting, responds, "I just want to be with you."

Now God is all in all. God sets the agendas, and we then see ourselves as God's servants and adoring subjects. God is sovereign, and we love it that way. God is still majesty and the end of all our beginnings, our longing, and our heart's desire, destination, and destiny. We are "lost in wonder, love, and praise." Yet, this too can be a dangerous phase, because the world, self, and all others can get lost in the ecstasy and zeal for God alone. The monk in his lofty tower who seeks only the image of God often misses himself and the beggar at the gate.

The danger in remaining in Mode III: Fanatical God-seeking, with no room to "love neighbor as thyself."

Mode IV: Love of Self for God's Sake

How can there be more? Is not Mode III the ultimate? No. The great, good gospel news is at this point or situation in our journey is that we <u>wake up and claim</u> the image of God <u>in us</u>. We experience God's <u>indwelling and immanent presence</u>. We are no longer distant, adoring from afar, with a vast gulf between earth and heaven. We discover God deep down inside. We live to be as we have been created and recreated in Christ: precious and redeemed, with our precious Redeemer living with us here and now.

How do we live with Christ? As friends. Jesus said, "I no longer call you servants but friends." This is Christ's ultimate plan for us! Can this be true? Can we find contentment with ourselves as we are, as God's adopted children and Christ's close companions? The best news is that divinity dwells in us! When we connect on this plane, accept, and embrace our salvation, our wholeness, we become overjoyed with our life in Christ.

This is Heaven on Earth. Heaven now. St. Augustine said, "None can become fit for the future life, who hath not practiced himself for it now." Beyond the door of death, I think the Heaven we encounter at that time will be more of the same in this time — loving companionship with God, with our neighbor (all Creation and all humanity) and with our self.

Is this self-centered? I don't think so. This is the reverse of self-centeredness. We are now in the stage of the "centered self" with God at our center, flowing from the depths of being, from a filled self. Our cups overflow, as a fountain filled from the springs of "living water" within. We live in Jesus, Love Himself, and "possessing this treasure in earthen vessels," with Christ's love overflowing through us to others in pure <u>Intercession.</u>

The danger in Mode IV: No real *Danger:* The risk is Ego death and selfishness. We gain selflessness instead, all for Christ's sake, and then find love, community, and more love. This is deliverance from conceit and a delicious danger worth any risk.

Living in intercessory community is where it all comes together for me. Almost all my encounters with the living God have been in company with other selves. The miracles of my life have been in the context of relationships. As Leo Tolstoy said, "He who desires to know the living God face to face should seek Him, not in the empty firmament of his mind, but in human love." As other beings, human and animal, have intersected with my own life, I have found God in those relationships. As I have been open to other living and loving beings, I have been open to God, as I understand God to be.

Intercession is praying for and with others, and each memorable moment of my own spiritual existence is populated with friends, Christian and non-Christian, young and old, of every race and many ethnic and cultural origins. To be in living, loving relationship with the living, and loving Christ is to be with a wealth of people, face-to-face and person-to-person.

I think Sartre said, "Hell is other people," but I have found the exact opposite. Heaven is other people in intimate companionship with Christ our Lord. That is what I celebrate, holding hands with many friends who have journeyed with me. I am thankful and look back with joy and gladness to the lands I have visited and the persons, animal and human, that I have known, Knowing that I do not need to gaze ahead at the helm into the distant horizon. It will be much the same to me, if good friends and dogs are there.

The Scripture that nourishes my journey is John 15:15-17. *"No longer do I call you servants, for the servant does not know what his master is doing; but I have called you friends, for all that I have heard from my Father I have made known to you. You did not choose me, but I chose you and appointed you that you should go and bear fruit and that your fruit should abide; so that whatever you ask the Father in my name, he may give it to you. This I command you, to love one another."*

Questions to ponder:

1. Have there been any special animals in my life? What were they? Have they taught you to love and be loved?

2. What blessings do you think these animals brought you? Name them to God.

3. If you haven't known any special animals yourself, if you were an animal, what animal do you think you might like to be? Why?

4. In the discussion of the four spiritual modes, where do you find yourself most often? Remember, we live in all four. Only God moves away from our selves to Christ.

5. Is there anyone in your life like the dog our little tale had God give Adam — admiring you, accepting you unconditionally, and just simply loving you for yourself? If not, you may want to begin praying for such a person to come into your life, praying to be able to recognize the person when he or she comes.

6. Has there been a person in your life who tormented you? How have you dealt with that abuse and cruelty? Has God helped you? Has a human or animal angel rescued you?

CHAPTER SIX

From Vulnerability
to Respect

—⚹—

Mystery Cats

From the same unreliable scroll: *After a while, it came to pass that Adam's guardian angel came to the Lord and said, "Lord, Adam has become filled with pride. He struts and preens like a peacock, and he believes he is worthy of adoration. Dog has indeed taught him that he is loved, but no one has taught him humility."*

And the Lord said, "I will create for him a companion who will be with him forever and who will see him as he is. The companion will remind him of his limitations, so he will know he is not worthy of adoration."

And God created Cat to be a companion to Adam. And Cat would not obey Adam. And when Adam gazed into the eyes of Cat, he was reminded that he was not the Supreme Being. And Adam learned humility. And God was pleased, and Adam was greatly improved. And Cat did not care one way or the other."

I originally heard these two dog and cat yarns told by Canon Paul Shoemaker at a church conference. He told me he found them on the internet. I have tried to track down the author with no success.

After using GOD and DOG as mirror images, I expected CAT and TAG to be in the feline story, but that is in my story instead. My experience with almost all cats is trying to play tag, or Catch Me If You Can. Perhaps I am too eager to suit a cat. Most of the cats I have known are introverts, and extroverts, like myself, make most introverts to run and hide. Yet introverts generally fascinate, mystify, and attract extroverts the way flowers attract bees.

Patches and Blackie, the only two cats I've ever known who came running when I called them, were extroverted, social and friendly. They acted like the dogs I have known —eager for approach, not given to avoidance and hiding. I enjoyed their attention but still obsessed over the other cats — the mysterious ones — that avoided me.

My friend and colleague, Herman Green, identifies this approach/ avoidance syndrome with the real-life behavior of a snake found in the Mid-Central U.S. called the blue racer. This snake will chase you if you run away and run away if you turn and pursue it. I am something of a blue racer myself, for when people turn from me or show indifference, my extroversion urges me to keep pursuing, talking, and trying to engage this reserved yet appealing person who has no interest in any engagement and only wants to be left alone. Only when I am sick do I want solitude.

In his great work on personality types, the psychotherapist Carl Jung coined the words "extroversion" and "introversion" to describe qualities he believed had existed in human beings from the dawn of human history.

In my own family, I certainly enjoy this outward-inward game. It makes for constant frustration with my grandchildren's pet cats, Mulder and Zenia. I can never catch either one, yet I keep on chasing them until I weary of the chase. Strange to say, after I have stopped my pursuit, they may come up to me when least expected and even less welcomed, demanding affection and stroking. Most cats are mysteries to me. Yet in spite of some of my wrong-headed ideas about cats, I have learned a great deal from them about boundaries.

My personable and extroverted daughter, Sandy, was blessed with a dog companion named Burt — a most beautiful, fluffy-white Alaskan Spitz. He was the soul of friendship and reflected the lively personality of his human guardian. Their personalities matched. Personality type may be more important than canine and feline differences, since all Sandy's animal pets are outgoing and possess generous portions of extroversion.

In my case as in Sandy's, when finding friends and nonromantic companions, the operative principle seems to be "like attracts like." My boyhood chums were much like me, full of extroversion. As I remember my closest friends, they were all outgoing, boisterous, friendly, talkative, funny, and fun. They all lifted my spirits and energized my life.

Nowadays my dear extraverted friend, Ron Thomson, is a tonic to my soul. Better than an antidepressant, by just being his entertaining and energetic self, he can quickly pull me out of the doldrums. More times than I can count, I have connected with Ron to receive his potion of pleasant good cheer. I often wonder if it is reciprocal. Once Ron's God-given joyfulness opens up my inner fountain and brings my own humor and vitality back to the surface, he too seems to enjoy the mutual response.

On the other hand, oddly enough, opposites do often attract when it comes to romance and our choice of lovers. My sweetheart for eternity, my wife, is almost my temperamental opposite—the sweetest, kindest introvert in my world. Not only has Ruth provided the subjective and thoughtful factors that I so often ignore, she has also rescued me from my own impulsiveness. She has never kicked my shins from under the table, but a sweet look of caution or a raised eyebrow is all I need to slow me down.

I am actually grateful for any helping glance or smile to remind me to listen more and talk less. Ruth is one of the best listeners I have ever known, and I have learned more of this art from her. I have often thought that her temperament is better suited for counseling than mine. In fact, I have often trusted her to do informal interviews for me and tell me her honest evaluations. We are a blessed example of two temperaments complimenting and supplementing each other. She loves dogs, but has wonderful cat like qualities.

Since my limited experience of cats has on the whole been the opposite of good cheer, my present view of them is rather like that of poor Adam in the fictitious Garden of Eden story. I am allergic to cats, their hair gets on my clothes, I get scratched, and they are indifferent and mysteriously quiet, reserved, and even unfriendly when approached. As with Adam, cats cut me down to appropriate size, and leave me properly diminished and quiet.

Yet, this has not been a curse. Being brought down to a level playing field is a blessing at times. Introverted cats and humans have often taken the wind out my sails when my sails were much too full of myself. I have learned, and keep relearning; that I seek out extroverted doglike friends when I want my conceit massaged and reluctantly receive introverted catlike persons into my life when I need confrontation.

I will never forget the time when I was telling Mike Collins, the headmaster of St. Mary's Hall, how pleased and excited I was over breaking a world Masters swimming record, "You're really full of yourself today, chaplain, aren't you?" he said softly and with a smile. What a crash to my soaring spirit. Yet how honest, caring, and helpful that one comment has been to me ever since.

Who was I kidding? I was fifty-five years old competing with other mid-life athletes. I had not broken the open world's record; I had only surpassed some other elders in swimming. It was only a big deal for me, hardly significant to a forty-year-old school administrator.

I now know that both ego comfort and confrontation are blessings. Like Adam, I rejoice to be approved, loved, and even adored, but I need accurate reality checks in order not to put myself in God's place at the center of my life. In recovery circles, the letters E.G.O. stand for "edging God out." Like all offspring of Adam and Eve, I may want affection and approval, but I also need humility and an honest acceptance of my human limitations. I also thank God for the blessings of all the honest cats in my life, feline and human.

It has been observed that a cat when a cat rubs against a human being, the cat is not saying, "I love you," but rather, "I love me and this feels good." I have no idea whether this is true, but I can accept it as a model of showing consideration to another living being in search of honest pleasure.

In comic strips, dogs were invariably portrayed as wise, entertaining, compliant, loyal, friendly, brilliant, or benign, while the cats were portrayed as sly, lazy, tough, crooked, contrary, or feisty. The stereotypes about dogs and cats seem to hold true even in the funny papers. Like all commonplace ideas and clichés, these probably reflect some prejudice as well as a good deal of truth.

I often encourage persons in Twelve-Step recovery programs to choose several sponsors. We all need many winners to listen and stick to; sponsors who share their own experience, strength and hope and tell their own story without giving advice.

In addition, we, like Adam, often need a cheer-leader — at least one sponsor of the "dog" type, who will comfort us, build up our diminished ego, and encourage with approval. Yet our greatest growth may come when we allow God to send us at least one other sponsor, of the "cat" type, who will confront us, tell it like it is, keep us humble and love us and care enough about us to be vigorously and rigorously honest. I have needed both. I still do.

All animals bless us, if we open ourselves to learn from them, and we would be especially deprived without the companionship of dogs and cats, the most popular pets. Boundaries are just one area where this learning can happen, as in the "Hula Hoops" exercise described below.

Boundaries

One of the workshops I am frequently asked to give has to do with boundaries. One of the first things I ask participants in a boundaries workshop to do is draw a map of their home state or country. Then we pass it around the group to see if we can guess each person's origins. All states, counties, cities, and countries have boundaries, prescribed limits, borders, and lines to mark one area from another. In my life-time, the boundaries of Europe have been redrawn several times. Some areas are still in dispute, such as the Golan Heights overlooking the Sea of Galilee, the West Bank, and numerous U.S. Congressional districts that will be redrawn as a consequence of the 2000 census.

A boundary is like a fence, wall, or hedge — a barrier to keep in and keep out. Nature provides lakes, rivers, oceans and mountains as given barriers. Humanity has built walls, fortresses and offshore limits to create its barricades in addition to natural ones. A case in point is the Rio Grande River, which divides Texas from Mexico but then flows right through New Mexico and up to Colorado without creating any demarcation between states.

All boundaries mark "this" from "that" as well as distinguishing "mine" from "yours." A boundary draws the line not to be crossed. Must human and animal disputes are turf wars of one kind or another — physical, sexual, mental, emotional, or behavioral. A moat around a castle is such a boundary-barrier. When Mexico wanted protection from the Comanche raids, they invited Stephen F. Austin to situate his new settlement between the Mexican settlers and the raiders of the plains. When this plan failed, the "Texicans" soon established themselves as a Republic and then as an annexed state of the United States, which by the Treaty of Guadalupe Hidalgo redrew the U.S. map, adding Texas, New Mexico, Arizona, Colorado, Utah, Nevada, and California. Right here in El Paso, where the Rio Grande River divides the United States from Mexico, the disputed Chamizal territory was finally settled in President John F. Kennedy's time.

When my wife and I visited Colorado's Mesa Verde, we were astounded at the advanced ancient civilization that lived on that plateau. More than 100,000 native people once inhabited that area.

One cliff dwelling, known today as the Cliff Palace, housed hundreds of men, women, children, dogs, and tame turkeys, but no domestic cats. Cats have been tough since ancient times and the cougars were too big and wild to tame.

These ancient people, who lived in naturally protected canyon caves facing south away from the winter winds, knew a great deal about boundaries and identifying themselves. Their clans, named for animals — bear, eagle, hawk, deer, elk, and bison — all had special characteristics, meanings, and markings that served as boundary signs as well.

We have much to learn from such sturdy people who lived on the cliff sides of the Southwest. Unlike the Plains Indians, they were more likely to understand and honor the territorial of other pueblos. For the most part, they abided by the healthy and helpful boundaries that are essential for safety, peace, and civilized life. Similar boundaries are honored by almost all animals as they mark their territory and keep out of each other's claims. Seldom do such animals wage war. We could learn from both the Pueblos and the animals.

A Boundary Demonstration
Hula Hoops

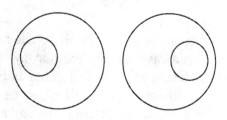

These circles represent the two Hula Hoops I keep in my counseling office to demonstrate the importance of boundaries in human relationships. Picture, if you will, a person inside each Hula Hoop, the two standing facing each other. When the distance is at least in the above position, each person's need for personal space does not usually feel violated. If each person holding the Hula Hoop around his or her back tried to reach out beyond the hoop, the hoops, or an outstretched arm could not touch. Of course when we want to be distant and beyond the range of polite conversation, our "hoops" with us inside are located even farther apart, like so:

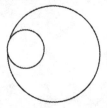 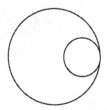

When both persons, by mutual permission, agree to communicate or interact from within the boundary protection of their respective Hula Hoops, ensuring that neither will intrude any farther than is acceptable, hoop A and hoop B can intersect, and each person shares some of the other's space.

Such boundary preservation, encroachment, or both come into play in all our realities — physical, emotional and sexual thoughts, feelings, wants, and actions. In the absence of invitation and agreement, no one has a right to cross over the Hula-Hoop line. Here is what friendly conversation would look like:

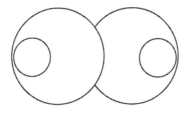

A more intimate relationship would look more like this, as each person becomes more comfortable and secure with the other:

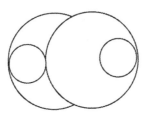

Note that this will be as close as two people with Hula Hoops up around their waists in the back can approach as they overlap. In the relationship shown here, the leading edge of each Hula Hoop can touch the other person's waist in front but go no farther. Therefore, we see that even when two persons come as close as touching, significant parts of the separate and individual persons are left untouched.

Without boundaries, two persons trying to interact would wind up inside each other's Hula Hoops, like dancing on another person's feet — enmeshed, fused, and lacking the freedom to move independently.

Sometimes a person who intrudes and invades another's space — taking off the healthy boundary of the "Hula Hoop" — may exchange it for a "lariat" by which to take hostages, reaching out into another's territory to lasso and control. The "Hula Hoop" preserves a person's personal power, just as a fence, hedge, or other protective enclosure protects and preserves one's private space at home. But someone intent on emotional pursuit and capture may set out to surprise an "unprotected" person — someone with porous boundaries or none — in order to take that person captive.

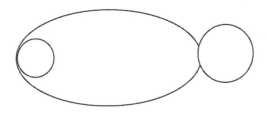

Cats have taught me a great deal about accepting other persons' "Hula Hoops," helping me to remember to keep my appropriate distance until invited closer, thus avoiding intrusion, interrupting, inserting myself, and taking anyone else "captive." The first skill to be learned by someone who wishes to avoid being taken "captive" is the simple word "NO." It may help to remember that "NO!" is a complete sentence!

In my own case, learning to accept negative responses and declare my own displeasure has been difficult. Over the last twenty years I have worked diligently at practicing saying "No" and risking rejection, as well as accepting "No" from others and enduring their rejection and disapproval. In relationships, the key is remembering that every person is always entitled to choose how he or she will respond to a given situation. I do not know why this should have been such a difficult learning, for really it is only common courtesy. Fortunately, I think I have finally achieved enough of this understanding of honoring others and myself so that I am able to model it and teach it as well.

When a person who tends to invade space has his or her Hula Hoop on — as Pia Mellody says, has their "boundaries on board" — that person <u>cannot</u> intrude, nor will he or she think it odd to be unable to get too close. That healthy boundary line will prevent crossing over the line. When a person who tends to allow intruders to approach too close learns to have an invisible Hula Hoop around his or her personal space, a protective barrier much like the force field on board the Starship *Enterprise* kicks in. Depending on the degree of the threat, the defensive shield can be employed with minimum, medium, or full force. Assertive protective measures assist everyone involved — the target to be invaded and the would-be invader.

Avoiding violations is always better than care-lessly blundering into dangerous territory. One thing is certain: if either person has his or her own invisible Hula Hoop securely in place, no invasion can take place. The shield will hold. If both have their hoops in place, it is doubly certain that intrusion cannot happen.

In the face of strong, repeated, or clever invasive attempts, personal Hula Hoops may have to become the equivalent of fortified walls. Making them so can and will both protect against victimization and restrain the attempted perpetration. Everyone bene-fits from clear boundary lines and well-guarded border crossings. One of the most valuable lessons we can instill into our children is how essential firm personal boundaries are, as protection against exploi-tation, violation or abuse.

As a boy in Panama, I played all over the massive 16-inch gun emplacements — powerful coastal artillery that would daunt any invader from setting foot on land. These guns could drive away any ship many miles from the shore. No one has ever tried to breach that massive defensive shoreline.

Some time back, at a workshop on sexual assault, I bought three T-shirts for my daughters with a message I had never seen before:

"Just what is it about NO that you don't understand?"

I'm told that most women have had the experience of sexually aggressive men rejecting their clear "No," apparently presuming that the woman really meant "Yes." My daughters tell me, and so have hundreds of counselees, that many men perceive such "warning shots" as challenges and simply will never take "No" for an answer. Perhaps this goes back into prehistory. Regardless of its origins, failure to respect another person's wishes is wrong and often even criminal, and the same principle applies for nations, races, and even animals captured and caged.

The sad history of humankind tells us that countries, groups, gangs, teams, cliques, and any human band can rape and pillage others. The weak invite the strong invader, while the well-fortified castle discourages invasion

One particular Scripture continues to remind me of the source of my real boundaries:

"For the Lord God is a sun and shield. He bestows favor and honor. No good thing does the Lord withhold from those who walk uprightly." (Psalm 84:11)

In addition, a second Scripture reminds me how to defend and equip myself:

> *"Therefore take the whole armor of God, that you may be able to withstand in that evil day, and having done everything, to stand firm. Stand therefore, fasten the belt of truth around your waist, and put on the breastplate of righteousness, as shoes for your feet put on whatever will make you ready to proclaim the gospel of peace. With all these, take the shield of faith, with which you will be able to quench all the flaming arrows of the evil one. Take the helmet of salvation, and the sword of the Spirit, which is the word of God."*
> (Ephesians 6:13-17)

Questions to ponder:

1. How comfortable do I feel when I must tell another person "No"? Remember Jesus urging our Yes to be Yes and our No to be No?
2. How comfortable do I feel when another person tells me "No"? Did Jesus always say, "Yes?"
3. Were there ever, or are there still, people in my life who disregard my wishes and personal space? Who are they, and how do they behave? Can I pray the Serenity Prayer, to change what can be and accept what cannot be, and the wisdom to know the difference?
4. In my relationships today, are there others — adults or children — whose wishes and personal space I may be violating? Can you ask them to tell you and accept their answer?
5. What are some of the places where I can begin to say "No" and make it stick with God's help?

CHAPTER SEVEN

From Selfishness to Serenity

—⚏—

We need help at times; indeed, even the most brilliant. It is so easy to forget the most obvious things in our recovery. We need little reminders from our friends. How easy is it to forget the slogan "I am Responsible" and start blaming others? It is also common to forget to "Live One Day at a Time" and rush into the future or ruminate about the past when all we have is Today. I suppose the easiest to forget is to "Let Go and Let God" as we struggle to manage our lives without Him.

The best such an example in my life was when I was writing <u>Letting God</u>. I had completed half the meditations and reached a roadblock. I could go no further. I complained to my wife that I was stuck and all dried up. She slyly asked, "What is the name of your book"? I replied, "You know, it's <u>Letting God</u>." She smiled and said, "Well, why don't you"? Oh, yes! It crashed in on me. Immediately, I stopped any more attempts to write and let God take over the job.

After three weeks of emptiness and impatience, ideas flooded my mind faster than I could process them. The last half was done in no time. I had forgotten. I stopped going to the real source of inspiration. It was so easy to forget.

Don't we need reminders in our walk? The Big Book of Alcoholics Anonymous is full of them. The Bible is too. Our friends in Christ and in recovery often jolt us into remembering. I think it is wise to recall that Jesus said, *"Do this in remembrance of me."*

However, Phillips Brooks said, "It is almost as presumptuous to think you can do nothing as to think you can do everything." Often we think in our ministry as well as our recovery, that we are completely unable to do anything at all. The truth is that we are powerless over our disease or our addictive compulsion, not everything. There are always possibilities along with impossibilities. Our job is to know the one from the other as the Serenity Prayer instructs us about acceptance and change. We almost always have choices, however. We do so much better if we stop trying to control what is out-of-control and turn that over to God in Christ. Yet, there is a lot left over that we can do and that God encourages us to do for ourselves. Thank God, we can look to ourselves for some power, some ability. We can read the scriptures, we can go to meetings, we can worship, we can meditate, we can pray, we can help others, we can even choose to adopt a positive attitude, more often than we would like to admit.

I am as certain as I can be that God does not expect us to do what we cannot do. Yet, he has blessed us with talents and gifts, especially our desires and longings, our hopes and our yearnings. Remembering that the word in Genesis is not literally *"living soul"* but rather *"living appetite"* and that we all are alive because of our appetites - for life, love, work, companionship and meaning. I like that and believe it. We need not learn or go into training in order to hunger, thirst and want. It seems God made us with aching desires crying out for fulfillment. I think it is this appetite that drives us to never give up, and makes it possible to choose to stick it out.

In my life, I have never seen it otherwise. We can choose to persevere and commit ourselves to the path of health and recovery or not. Our determination is determined by this innate God-given appetite within ourselves and by no one else. Isn't this so true when the opposite takes place, and we see our friends lose their appetites and will to live?

Josh Billings said, "Consider the postage stamp: its usefulness consists in the ability to stick to one thing till it gets there." I think that is the way it works. Jesus was quite clear in his story about the persistent woman who kept on knocking on the judge's door late at night, until he got up and answered her request. St. Paul urges us to never grow weary in our prayers and to pray in and out of season. Being insistent and persistent is the course that God in Christ has set before us and he knows we can do this. Distinguishing what we can manage and then trusting that God-given capacity will give us encouragement in our limited abilities. Added to God's unlimited power this will produce a bountiful harvest, if we never give up on ourselves and God.

Living in faith is not an easy task. Yet, we do not have a hard taskmaster. We have a hard lover...our master - Jesus our Lord and Savior. His love and the love he creates in us will continue to lead and to heal. This is the essence of his kingdom, in which we serve as his loyal subjects.

As we all know, love is a hard act, not an easy feeling. Yet Christ showed us how – he loved to the end, even as the nails were driven into his body. This love lives in us too. It is his plan. His miracle of love is a mystery of "tough acts." The difficult path of caring for and ministering to others, sharing and daring with others, is not easy but it always creates healing and hope. Love is never turned aside but keeps on keeping on. May we depend on this love. May we grow strong in this love.

The Solitary Self

Fifteen years ago, I finally kept a promise to myself that I had made some twenty years earlier. Having long admired the great Christian mystics of the past, I wanted an inward meditative experience of my own. For years I had struggled half avoiding and half seeking - "a silent and solitary spiritual retreat." Finally, the opportunity for such an alone time confronted me. Finally, I was face to face with a full week to enter into solitude with myself and with God. No more excuses. I would "be still and know God" as never before. Moreover, if you knew me personally, you would know what a difficult thing that would be.

The place and time presented themselves. The setting was perfect. By accident or by providence, I found my "chapel" — the Hassayampa Bird Sanctuary in Wickenburg, Arizona, during the hottest part of summer. I had noticed the road signs pointing to the sanctuary many times as I commuted to the Meadows Treatment Center, where I was participating in a counselor-training course. Eventually curiosity compelled me to investigate this sanctified place. Perhaps this "church for birds" would be my place, my refuge and my chance to be on retreat.

What I found could not have been more inviting and appropriate. No one else was there. The Nature Conservancy, who owned the place, had temporarily closed it to the public. Yet, to my surprise, the resident caretaker agreed to let me come in each day and stay for as long as I wanted, between sunrise and sunset.

I wandered through the preserve at will, marveling at the lush foliage of this riparian forest and the countless birds everywhere. What better place and time to spend an entire week in meditation and prayer? Yet, I had my doubts. As a boy, I had wantonly shot birds with my BB gun. As an adult, I had hunted quail, duck and dove. Was this God's way of forgiving me? Was I being invited into this home for birds as a way of welcoming me as a friend now and no longer an enemy? I was hoping so. I accepted the invitation.

Within this small preserve of just a few acres I came upon a small meadow sheltered by native cottonwood and wild willow trees, under the shadow of a cactus-covered mountain and refreshed by a rivulet of crystal-clear water. I experienced a new spirit of optimism at the promise the place seemed to hold. I prayed I would find serenity and a restored soul in this green pasture, beside these still waters. Yet, my fear of being alone and lonely was still with me. I felt anxious at the thought of a weeklong retreat.

The truth was that I felt less fearful than just plain tired. At that time in my life, after twenty years of parish ministry, I was feeling depleted. I was thoroughly fed up with talking, preaching, doing, working, worrying – yes, even praying. I was caught up in one activity after another, a captive to schedules, meetings and agendas.

In addition, I had let the same unhealthy pattern bleed over into my so-called vacations. Even my vacations wore me out with too much doing, seeing, and traveling. Feeling like frenetic Phil, I did have sense enough to know that I needed peace and Sabbath time. Nevertheless, I did not know how to calm down enough to be still. All I seemed to be able to achieve was more layers of anxiety.

At the time that I discovered the Hassayampa sanctuary, I still had one week to go of a two-week training program. "Enough of training programs, enough of any kind of work!" I cried out to the birds in the trees. "I want to rest!" I uttered my solitary protest while gazing on one the most beautiful spots I had ever seen. An assurance came to me. I sensed that somehow I would find my true self in this stream-side seat of peace, under a canopy of cooling leaves that protected me from the July heat. I canceled the last week of the training program, but I stayed on in Wickenburg.

Although the stream was a mere trickle, just a stretch of seeping water with small still pools here and there, seemingly pitifully inadequate to sustain such a massive stand of trees, it was called the Hassayampa River. How could this be a river? I could easily step across it. Soon I learned that the name was a Native American word meaning "the river that flows on its back," because most of this lengthy "river" is dry on the surface, with very little water above ground. Yet below the surface flows an aquifer vast enough to help Phoenix become an oasis. Flowing on underground, below the desert sands, this seemingly insignificant river is actually massive enough to supply wells, ponds, even lakes, wherever it is tapped.

Learning this, I recalled my life back in Texas. San Antonio's great metropolis has a tiny river, yet is also fed by the Edwards Aquifer, a river flowing underground. I now live on the southern part of the narrow Rio Grande, which is fed by the snows of Colorado and also has an unseen aquifer underground. Such rivers that flow on their backs are not uncommon, but it would have required far more than one step to cross the San Antonio River, or the Rio Grande.

The "river" of my spirit was on its back too, upside down, only coming to the surface here and there. Most of the time, I felt like a dry riverbed, arid or barely damp. I had never stopped to think that beneath my barrenness, invisible, was a limitless reservoir of living water. Until then, my own spiritual "water" had seemed to be buried deep below the surface, hundreds of feet underground, attainable only through solid rock. Like a mesquite tree that has to sink its taproots deep down through rocky ground to find refreshment, I had imagined I would have to dig my way desperately into the bowels of the earth to find water for my thirsty roots.

Thirst and a New Baptism

I remembered complaining to a clergy friend about that time that I felt like an empty pipe, existing merely to carry the water of grace to others, and that only someone else's turn of the faucet could fill me. When there was no one to bless, comfort, help or guide, I felt hopelessly empty. Stifling tears, I asked "Why isn't there a little basin or a small amount in the pipe for me?" I expected sympathy or at least some sensitivity to my dejection. What I got back was, "That's your job, Phil, to be a channel for others." I realized that he was in worse shape than I. He never stopped flowing. I asked the wrong person. I stopped asking.

With no satisfying answer to my need for a refreshing drink of spiritual water, as I gazed at the tiny stream in front of me, I saw a baptismal basin— just for me. An Episcopalian can do with just a little poured water. and need not be immersed. I surely needed a fresh baptism of the spirit. I was ready to plunge into a deep pool of spirituality. I felt somehow quite close to Peter when he tried to refuse the foot washing from Jesus, who finally replied, *"Lord, not my feet only, but also my hands and my head!" (John 13:9)* Immersion was my goal. Diving deeply was my desire.

To my embarrassment and pain, I had once snorkeled down to a piece of coral in Hawaii, and although it almost made my ears pop from the pressure, I persevered and retrieved the prize. I gave the coral to a friend. Later I felt guilty for damaging a living reef just for personal and selfish treasure, even for someone else.

This time I was just as determined on a spiritual level, during this summertime seclusion, to go all the way - down deep to find the living water of Christ, the pearl of great price, despite the pain or water pressure. I hoped I would not be treading or intruding where I did not belong. Scripture often refers to "the deep" as a dimension of dread and death, a realm to avoid. Nevertheless, at this time I was ready to die in order to live.

As a lifetime swimmer, I love the water and often tell folks, "I am no good on dry land." I have started many a race down from the starting blocks. Here there was no pool to dive into, yet somehow I felt the same excitement. The adrenaline was the same. Was this puddle of water to become my most important race toward nativity and newness?

Just before this time I had served as rector of St. Thomas the Apostle Church where once at a parish carnival, I was the designated victim in a dunking booth. That was fun and refreshing. I hit the water often. I loved staying under as long as I could and then I jumped up with glee and raucous laughter.

Now I was just as eager to be dunked in this spot, to immerse my being here. I yearned to be baptized anew, all the way under, as many times as it took. Maybe my surfacing would be just as joyfully boisterous. Philip, the Episcopalian, was ready to go Baptist. I prayed for the drowning death in Baptism, so that I could arise, dripping from the water, into Eucharistic fellowship afresh and anew.

However, it was getting hot, now over 100 degrees. I went back to the hotel to cool off. At sunrise the next day, borrowing the folding luggage rack from the room along with a pillow to use as a seat, I drove back in the cool desert morning to what became my God spot. I would spend each morning there during six more days of serious solitude.

A Coyote Couple

Soon I was to know myself blessed beyond measure. What I learned on the banks of the Hassayampa transformed my life. I was in place and ready for the sunrise the next morning, seated on my pillowed luggage rack, gazing across the tiny stream toward the opposite bank. What I saw gave me the worst case of "buck fever" I had yet felt – the pounding pulse of discovery you feel when spotting your quarry. Both hunters and photographers experience it. There, peeking back at me through the underbrush, were two coyotes. When they saw me sitting motionless just a few feet from them, they froze. I too was transfixed and on alert.

Nevertheless, I had to breathe and I stirred. They spotted me, and then they sniffed in my direction. I expected them to run back into the brush. Fearless and apparently accepting my obvious presence, they surprised me. They looked directly at me, came up to the water, and drank until they were satisfied. They stayed almost within my reach until finally they turned and disappeared back into the bushes. A few minutes later, I could see them moving up the cactus-carpeted mountain beyond. I sat in wonder, feeling like a modern day Adam in the Garden of Eden. My spirit was moved as well as soothed.

Above me, the trees were alive with birds waking to the new day, singing and darting in every direction. With a sense of blessing and joy, I wanted to join in their songs. A holy moment had come to me, and even now, I still am inspired when I remember and relive this grace. I too left my nest and with the birds arose to greet the new day. Strolling down every path of the preserve, reading the names of the labeled trees and seeking out each species of bird, I spent the rest of the morning trying to digest this epiphany, this theophany taking place.

What had just happened? Were the coyotes and the birds angels sent to bless me? Who could answer that but God? Why had the coyotes not fled? They were not afraid. Maybe the wily pair was too thirsty to be afraid. Perhaps they were used to humans at their drinking trough. Yet, I could not help but thank them for not running from me. I had a sense of being invited, accepted and included in this lovely garden. Perhaps the coyotes and the birds were being hospitable to me – the foreigner in their country.

Were the birds singing to me? Of course not. They were just busy getting on with the day's necessary search for food and feeding. Yet, I thank God for their presence and their song. Like many other seekers of the divine, I had asked, knocked, sought, and was graced with having new answers given and new doors opened to a new life discovery. The priceless gift of serenity became real and immediate. How and why are not important to me now. My emptiness was gone. It vanished. I felt full, refreshed, renewed and transformed from within "the deep" as well as "from above." Though I wanted to leap and dance, my feet stayed planted, while my soul sang and danced. The inexplicable holy and I had met each other again.

The next day I came back with a camera and took a roll of photographs of this holy spot. I still have my favorite picture of this sacred scene before me as I write. The many meanings of this experience are too rich to digest. Yet of one thing I am certain: I came to this place troubled and in turmoil, and peace and refreshment found me and finds me much more often now. Something sacred and deeply moving had stirred me. To this day, my Hassayampa time remains an encouraging boost to my on-going refreshment. Yet, even such a "born again" experience was not enough I soon found out.

The Social Self

My love for all of life and all that lives was ignited on this puny riverbank I had always loved animals, but that day my love for animals and all of nature was deepened and intensified. I wanted to embrace not only all human beings but all life as well. Mysteriously, I felt connected. I no longer felt lonely, although I was without any human company.

I felt invited into that refuge, into that wildlife sanctuary, for a purpose. Day after day, I came, and although at the beginning I felt that I had to walk, read, and talk aloud, by the end I had become able just to sit and allow my surroundings to sink silently in. Finally in those last two days, unity superseded individuality and independence. My solitary existence and self-concern were being integrated into a larger sensitivity to others and to all of life.

Nature and the natural had come to my rescue, bestowing the gift of closeness and love. Connection, combining, linking, and coming together restored my lonely soul. I sensed a wonderful welcome, an invitation to include more life and more living beings in my selfish existence. Affiliation and comradeship beckoned, and I responded. John Donne's famous words about no one being an island, but a part of the main, described this new state of my spirit. Now I was feeling a part of all creation, no longer apart from it.

What seized me with the greatest power of connection came from the coyote couple. As I witnessed those two wily ones become trusting of me and move to the streamside to drink, my immediate mind-picture was of my wife and myself. I became intensely aware of Ruth, my life mate. "Two by two" entered my musings. Whenever I am away from my wife or she away from me, I seem weaker, uncertain, and lacking the confidence I have with her.

Perhaps, the sight of a wily human would have easily spooked a lone coyote. It is harder for me to trust and risk without my mate, as I have learned to lean on her for support and appreciation. It is vastly easier for me to venture forth with my soul mate than face adventures alone. Moreover, for any of us, "we" is better than "I." God made us to be independent, resourceful and self-reliant, yes, but never caught up in thinking we can do and control it all. I believe we always need a lot of help from our friends.

Having been blessed at the Hassayampa by a new awareness of community and a fresh communion, I knew that to be authentic I could never remain on a solitary path. Doing so would be contrary to my true nature. The notion of going it alone became unthinkable. I came away with a fresh appreciation of my life as a married man, as a father and as a companion.

"Just look at those two coyotes," I thought, struck by their couple-ness. Then I began to consider the birds and their partners. I knew that coyotes mate for life, and that many birds stay with their mates for life as well — for example, the Canada goose. Mutuality and marriage were defining my being anew. Perhaps distance does make the heart grow fonder, for I suddenly was overcome with a great yearning for my wife. I longed for her presence, ached to share this holy place with her. I could hear myself repeating the words from Genesis: *"It is not good that the man should be alone."* (Genesis 2:18) I actually felt envious of the lovebirds in the air and the coyote couple beside the stream. I also imagined that the coyotes had some pups back in their den, and that the bird nests were full of young fledglings. I missed my marvelous daughters right along with their mother.

Suddenly, in a new way, I had become truly one with Ruth. I could no longer be separate, independent, solitary. My identity had become partner, father, and friend. A solo life was no longer my calling. At that moment, I knew that solitude did not describe my authentic state. Although I had imagined that a silent retreat, a withdrawal alone and away from the world was a worthy and desired goal, when I tried to make it happen the first thing I experienced was togetherness!

My appreciation for the people and even the pets in my life became enhanced. I knew that to be authentic I could never be a hermit. While detachment was not my thing, attachment definitely is. Solitude brought me the blessings at the Hassayampa, but not as a permanent state. I am a mate, a colleague, and any feelings of loneliness represent an urge to move toward my wife and my friends. I was grateful to recall that another solitary man named Jesus not only sought out friends and disciples, he depended upon them and still does.

Paradoxically, when I left Wickenburg to return to Texas, I wanted to stay and go at the same time. I wanted to continue drinking the spiritual water that was connecting me to this larger life, yet I knew I was no longer personally thirsty or truly empty. I was eager to go home to my beloved wife and family. What I had experienced was enough.

Wanting more, yet needing no more, is a mystery—possibly the most enduring mystery of the spiritual life. Perhaps this is the priceless gift of serenity. Perhaps this is what Jesus meant when he said, *"Those who drink of the water that I will give them will never be thirsty. The water that I will give will become in them a spring of water gushing up to eternal life."* (John 4:14)

Rehydration

Apparently, my dose of the living water was exactly the right one. Any more might have been an overdose of joy. I found I could not experience happiness without feeling the urge to share it with my companions in life. I knew I could always return to this God spot, for the Hassayampa Sanctuary is within me now, and I can flee to it like a bird any time I choose.

It is not far away. It is everywhere, and it is full of life. It is a vibrating, populous realm of *"angels and archangels and all the company of heaven."* In this wonderful creation, empty pipes are filled, and disconnected folks connect. . That was the main angelic message of the birds: why be alone and lonely when so many of us are singing and living and enriching us all? I could hear Jesus' words from Scripture *"I came that they might have life and have it abundantly."* (John 10:10) as a song from the treetops and the desert with a chorus of "Welcome, brother!"

As I continued to reflect on my transforming retreat, I treasured a saying from the Jewish tradition that Bishop Terence Kelshaw shared: "Joy is Peace dancing, and Peace is Joy resting." Since that week in Arizona, I have never forgotten to dance and to rest. Nor have I ever forgotten that joy and peace are forever linked. In my pre-Hassayampa days, I was out of balance. Dancing to a compulsive tune to please and achieve, I had no joy in such a dance. Rest was impossible, and so was peace. The dance I was dancing was a dance of death, because I was dancing with myself alone. I could not stop long enough to be blessed or receive the hand of another to dance with me. God cut in, sweeping aside my puny concerns and reintroducing me to the grace of partnership, appreciation, companionship, and friendship with the Source of my being, with all God's creatures and all God's children.

What I learned from the upside-down river is that the source of life flows on within us in spite of all perception of barrenness and barriers in our lives. I discovered that I am not a lonely mesquite tree, seeking deep wells, but rather a wild willow seeking other willows to become groves nourished by ever-available water. I discovered that rarely do we have to hew out wells from solid rock to find healing. It is not that strenuous, nor is it that lonely. The water we need is close by, in the life all around us, in the everyday-ness of our families, friends and neighbors — and in the communities of love and faith. As a great Asian sage said, "A person going in search of God is like a fish going in search of water."

This is why the church family and Twelve-Step recovery groups mean so much to me. Although far from perfect, the church has been, and continues to be, my primary community, enhanced by Twelve-Step fellowships. In both families I have learned to appreciate differences without having to differ, distinctiveness without disapproval, contrast without contrariness, equality without equivalence, being dissimilar without dissimulation, and standing alone without being aloof or lonely.

Balance

I appreciate the balance between and need for independence and interdependence in my life, but I know that to be myself, I resonate more with closeness than with distance. I enjoy "me and mine" some of the time, but I can never be me without "we and ours." Although I enjoy my separateness at times, in small doses, I find dancing cheek-to-cheek and with joined hands, much more appealing than performing a solo, or dancing far removed from my partner.

Many people enjoy their differences and their independence more than their connections, but that is only right and good as each of us finds our natural, true, and real selves in life. God has given us all the freedom to do our own balancing act. My bird experience helped me also see that a one-winged bird is out-of-balance and cannot fly. Moreover, an individual tilting too much one way stumbles. I have found my two wings: an authentic self and a beloved companion. Self, neighbor and God - a body with two wings that can fly.

After my Hassayampa retreat, a new trust in others began to pervade my counseling practice, so that I undertook to listen respectfully to whatever folks said up front before deciding to dig deeper into anyone's life. Generally nowadays, I decline to second-guess anyone and simply honor the "chief complaint" exactly as the people in distress who come to me for counseling frame it, before I start any uncovering process of my own.

So much healing is close at hand, if we will only look and see, stop, listen and join in. Today I offer my hand and a partnership to my counselees while we team up to solve problems. I try to travel with those who seek my guidance, so that we walk together to find health, healing, and wholeness. We are fellow pilgrims on this journey. God and his healing love are always available "*in the midst of two or three who come together in his name.*"

Questions to ponder:

1. What is your deepest desire in life? God? Health? Love? Companionship? Peace? All of the above?

2. Does that desire have to do with a greater closeness to others? Does it have to do with a greater closeness to God?

3. What might you do to help your deepest desire be fulfilled? Pray? Search scripture? Seek personal guidance?

4. Is there someone you might ask to journey with you in seeking that fulfillment—for example, a good friend, or someone who could be a spiritual friend?

5. Are you a solitary type, or are you always in a crowd? In either case, do you suppose you might benefit from seeking a greater balance in your life?

CHAPTER EIGHT

From Grief to Gratitude

—w—

Failure and frustration have been a significant part of my walk in Christ. Most of it has been disposed of through the grace of God. It has taken years to learn to keep trusting and keep walking the talk and following the way.

More than twenty years ago, I went along with a friend to his hunting camp near Laredo, Texas. It was a beautiful ranch, full of wildlife, mesquite trees, cactus and brush. I loved it. I usually fished in the well-stocked ponds, called "tanks" in Texas, since they were really stock tanks for the cattle that shared the range with the deer, javelina, bobcats, and quail.

My first night in the cabin I got little rest. All through the night, I heard a rustling, skittering sound not far from me in the darkness. There was no electricity. The camp lanterns were extinguished, and everyone else in the cabin was sound asleep. So I managed to sleep only during the periods when I was able to convince myself that whatever was out there in the dark was not going to join me in my lower bunk.

When morning finally dawned, I sleepily reached for my boots and found both of them filled to the brim with corn! Puzzling over the strange sight of corn-filled boots, I was told by my host that a pack rat was busy storing corn it had found in one of his feed sacks. As I poured the feed corn back into the pilfered sack, I actually felt sad. What a picture of frustration! I imagined being that little creature, working so long and hard through the night, and then tried to imagine how grieved I would have been after filling two large boots, just to see the corn poured right back in the sack. How like the many losses we all experience in life.

I could not help empathizing with the defeat that little rodent must have felt. Although I cannot prove it, any more than I can prove the existence of God, I believe animals have real feelings, and emotions purer and less complicated than ours. Even if I am wrong, I prefer to honor all creation with this assumption and respect. Believing that all living things have feelings, I become sensitive, respectful, and caring about anything alive.

The sense of loss and grief brought on by frustrated efforts must therefore be common to all living beings. My own experiences have provided me ample pain from loss and disappointment, and most of the suffering was unexpected. A very wise man said that when things are going well, watch out and watch your back – there might be a knife soon to be planted there.

Our Paradise Found

A few days after my encounter with God and my true being at the upside-down river in Arizona, Ruth and I met up with another "paradise found." My bishop asked if I would entertain an invitation to become rector of a wonderful small church in a small community, located in what we thought was a valley of paradise. I had lately concluded that counseling individuals, couples and even families was my calling for the rest of my days. If I were to become a rector of a congregation, this opportunity for professional counseling would be limited. I would have to give up my hard-earned career as a psychotherapist and chaplain.

For eight years, God had given me a ministry in the community to suffering persons as well as a blessed relationship with young people at St. Mary's Hall as chaplain and confidant. I was uneasy about leaving this rich life of service and consequent appreciation. Yet, this small friendly church was so appealing to Ruth and me that I accepted the bishop's request.

So we left the home we had built in San Antonio, complete with a seventy-five foot lap pool, to journey an hour's drive north to a village just south of Austin. It was indeed a paradise, a true heaven on earth. We lived in a small rented cottage next to a lovely ranch. Deer, turkey, quail and other wild creatures bedded down in our enormous front yard. We could walk with our dog to a stream shaded by gigantic cypress trees. The people were as genuinely friendly and accepting as any, we had ever met.

I was soon to celebrate twenty-five years in the ministry. This calling was perfect. It was a dream come true. Here we would spend the rest of our days, retiring here along with other clergy, who also loved this lovely valley village. We were surrounded by wildlife, warm people, welcoming arms and willing souls, eager to team up together with me in nurturing service to others in that small part of God's kingdom.

With energy I did not dream I had, I worked hard and long to lead and work with the leaders and members of the church. We were able to reach out to many unchurched persons. I was able to visit almost every home and small business where members lived. We participated in the many wonderful activities the church provided. Sunday attendance increased. The small chapel was full. We were sure we were in paradise.

Our Paradise Lost

A year later we were gone, unvalued, unappreciated. Even today, Ruth and I cannot fathom what happened. About nine months into our ministry there, I found myself under attack for personal failures. Nothing I could say would defuse the church leaders' ire or diminish their disappointment at my alleged failings. At a final meeting with these leaders, even a professional pastoral counselor and group facilitator could not deter or open avenues to reason, repair and reconciliation. The facilitator left the meeting dejected and frustrated, leaving me and my wife to continue to face accusations and attacks on our honesty. There was no willingness to listen or check out the unsubstantiated charges they made, which could have been easily proven mistaken. However, their minds were made up and closed.

To a person, the twelve persons on the church board rejected and disapproved of me as a person and a leader. Our dreams were dashed. Paradise was lost. Confused and in despair, the day after I was confronted with the help of my friend, Keith Miller, I entered a Christian hospital as a safe haven for treatment for acute clinical depression. I stayed three weeks, found my emerging true self and tendered my resignation to the bishop as rector of the village church.

My good friend, Ron Thomson, found an opening for me as a counselor in El Paso, where I could be true to my vow made at the Hassayampa River. There is an old saying, "When one door closes, another one opens." It was surely true for me. I did visit the little church a few weeks after my resignation to conduct a funeral. At that time an old friend remarked, "You certainly landed on your feet, Father." If ever I doubted God's providence, this experience wiped away all doubt. What is important to me now is that I am home – safe in a new haven.

George MacDonald spoke for me when he said, "We learn that the storms of life have driven us, not upon the rocks, but into the desired haven." My entire life since childhood has shown me over and over that apparent tragedies turn into triumphs. St. Paul's words of comfort have confirmed and rati-fied each experience when he said; *"We know that all things work together for good for those who love*

God, who are called according to his purpose." (Romans 8:28)

These last fifteen years have been a true paradise for us where person and place are "meet and right" and fit the gifts God has given me and I am so grateful that God never stops working good in all our lives.

What I experienced in the village church brought on a grief the likes of which I have never known before or since. I had never felt so stupid and inadequate, even at my own father's hands. I was not wanted! We shall no doubt always have the wounds, or at least the scars, yet the wonder is that today we are at peace, with no blame to place – unless it is to say that I was naïve, blind and operating in a dream world. I should have known after twenty-five years that people judge, condemn, find fault, listen to rumors and gossip and sincerely believe it all. We all do this without thinking or checking out the facts. I am sure in my own conceit and confidence I had sown some of the seeds that turned out weedy. If I did, I surely did not know it. No one even hinted at any problems. I was blind-sided.

Still reeling and grieving the loss of our dreamland, Ruth and I came to find welcoming arms and loving friends here in the desert, friends who have rarely let us down. After just a few weeks after moving here, Ruth had to battle a life-threatening illness and was surrounded and held up by (as Ruth calls it) "a pillow of love."

We still visit other friends in the valley village, friends who were no part of our rejection and dejection and would have resisted, even combated the leaders' actions. I did leave by choice and refused to become an issue that would split the church. My resignation shocked the majority of the church since they had no idea what was going on behind the scenes. Our own experience was a terribly sad one; yet sadder still is the fact that few of our old friends attend the little church anymore.

Paradise Regained

The final outcome was one of self-finding. I finally met my true self and found one of life's greatest joys. As I have said elsewhere, 'when any of us can be face to face with our own souls and see the right and real person looking back at us, the event is rare and wondrous.' I thank God for my village experience today. I am so grateful.

My own experience of grief has given me an appreciation for the grief and mourning so many others have over lost dreams and paradises. I may have been living in a fool's paradise, yet loss is loss and it creates grief, with all its stages and states of being. I am grateful to God to be back with myself as one who cares for and can bleed with others in their sadness as a wounded healer, who knows that joy follows despair.

Moving through Grief

One of the most moving scenes in *The Man from La Mancha* came as Don Quixote lay dying and was roused by his lady Dulcinea to hear the words of the song, "The Impossible Dream" again.

"Tell me the words," he asks.

"But they are your words, my Lord," she responds.

He remembers then and sings the magnificent song that embodied his dream.

The Seven T's of Moving through Grief

For years at funerals and during times of loss and grief, I have shared with those who are in the midst of their mourning these blessings that God gives us to cope with our sorrow and pain. *Tears, Talk, Touch, Time, Toil, Trust, and Thanksgiving*. In my heart-break, my own words of comfort returned to me as a benediction of grace. It was as if I heard an owl say, "They are your own words, Philip. Listen to them."

With Ruth's help and the support again of my dear friend, Keith Miller, I was able to embrace and allow my *tears* to flow. *Talk* became an outlet and way of trying to understand what God wanted for me in this crisis. *Touch* became so real as my loved ones and friends hugged and comforted me. *Toil* became an escape from the pain, as I threw myself into the writing of a new book. *Time* itself as it passed, moment by moment and day by day, provided healing. *Trust* began to envelop me as I was enveloped by love and care. Finally, *Thanksgiving* for the whole wrenching experience became real for me as I rejoiced in the healing and compassionate way those

I trusted treated me. All the seven T's helped me as they can help anyone in grief.

Once when I was giving a talk on these seven T's, I asked for any more words the group could think of. One man laughed and joked, "Why not Tylenol, tacos and tequila?" This was good for a hearty laugh all around. In fact, it is commonplace to see well-meaning clergy; physicians, relatives or friends urge a grieving person to fall back on sedatives, tranquilizers or sleeping pills.

However, I am so glad I did not dull my senses with painkillers, comfort myself with food or immerse myself in alcohol. Grief is a natural experience, and when we deaden ourselves with food or mind-altering substances, we cheat ourselves of the richness and healing that can come through immersion in the grieving process. The way out of grief is through it not around it. How much better, as we grieve, to rely upon the natural gifts of God and the promise that his gracious healing will come.

As we look for God's comfort in each sob, in our speaking, in each passing second, in every supportive squeeze, in the new trust that the sun will shine again and finally in thankful satisfaction that accepts all the pain, we are getting well and back into well being. When personal pain is offered to God's honor and love, saving health is the invariable outcome. The early Christians considered it an honor to suffer for Christ. One of my mentors called such moments "our cross time" and should be expected if we love the Lord. Living in such saving health is where I am today and I look forward to more blessings in whatever circumstances I am found.

Grief and Depression

As I remained under a psychiatrist's care for over a year after my painful resignation of the village church, I discovered that most of what I went through was natural grief with some clinical depression thrown in. I hasten to add that grief is not necessarily depression, although mourning a loss is a depressing experience. As a counselor who has ministered to both grief and depression, including my own, I can add some insights.

Every normal person experiences loss and grief. Not everyone has clinical depression, which is an illness, an affective disorder – affecting our feelings. Grief is a reaction to events, people and things that are usually obvious. The losses of a job, friend, relative, place or position are disappointments that make sense and connect to reality. We can put our finger on those things.

Depression may not make any sense at all and come upon the afflicted person for no good reason at all, when everything that is obvious is rosy. Most grief is an intense response to a well-known phenomenon, such as death and major loss. Depression can overshadow a person with grayness, lack of desire to live, pessimism, deep sadness, loss of appetite and energy, no interest in usual pleasures and routines, incessant crying or none at all, confusion, over-eating and more often than we know – despair, that leads to suicide attempts and suicide.

Although the grieving person may feel any or all of the above, grief does not last forever. Although depression is treatable and beatable, many depressed persons may never feel normal or ever know what normal happiness is. A grieving person usually finds joy again, although it may take a year or two. Whereas medication is only a temporary relief for the initial stage of grieving, a physician's skillful prescriptions and counsel can give necessary and long-lasting help to the depressed.

A few months after my grief was over, my need for depression medication ended. I continue to check in with my doctor, Dan Blunk, for continued diagnosis and medication if needed. My depression, as most depressed persons, is linked to a chemical imbalance that I am prone to, in good times and bad. The bad times may make my depression worse or even set it off. However, only a skilled psychiatrist can sort out the real clinical differences between grief and depression. I knew I was depressed and in grief. Someone else may not know. In my case, my hospitalization was helped primarily by my hospital doctor, Tracy Gordy. My recovery from grief was assisted mostly by my Christian spiritual director, who helped restore my faith and trust in God.

I would recommend anyone who is sad, down and despairing about anything or anyone to see *both* a psychiatrist and a spiritual counselor. Neither condition is one to tough out alone. No one is ever hurt by good and godly counsel, whether from science or religion. They have gone hand-in-hand in my life.

In fact, though different in diagnosis, both grief and depression can be helped by the seven T's. Tears, talking, touching, time, toiling, trusting and thanking can be responses and processes that never hurt, but in depression's case, they may not be enough and only a proficient psychiatrist or counselor can help heal the illness in depression.

Don and Diane's Dilemma

I had only renewed my practice of counseling for a few weeks, when I was able to put my empathy and crushing personal experience into good use with one of the first couples who came to me. My own grief over communication failures and misunderstandings has connected me since then to many couples caught in the same difficulties. All the feelings that flow from loss and let frustration come gushing out, especially anger, ranging from irritation to rage.

Moreover, these couples, in addition to grief, frequently are also feeling loneliness, guilt, shame, regret, and disgust, pain or fear. At the beginning of the therapeutic work, they may not be able to identify their feelings or emotions, as I could not, but through appreciative sharing with understanding helpers, all of us can learn to call these feelings by their true names.

No one seems to enjoy such impasses and difficulties. Yet, few couples with communication defects find them easy to repair. Wise couples seek out help through books, workshops, television, and advice from friends and pastors. Some may seek out the counsel of marriage and family therapists. I needed hospitalization to get my life back. Help is always there for us all if we *"ask, search and knock."* (Matthew 7:7)

A couple among all the many couples coming to me for help, the one that appeared to be the most frustrated with their ability to communicate was Don and Diane. At the far fringes of middle age, they both were both miserable in their marriage, for their conflict had been ongoing for more than ten years. Marital therapists refer to such couples as – "conflict habituated," in habitual discord. I experienced their discord and mutual discontent immediately. During the entire first session, they seemed a caricature of a married couple doing and saying all the wrong things. From the start, they guaranteed communication failure with every word, gesture, and facial expression.

Making every glaring communication error in the book, Don and Diane abandoned courtesy and respect, engaged in verbal attacks, blamed and accused, made repeated you-statements, pointed their fingers, sneered, ridiculed, used sarcasm, did not listen, and dumped their frustration and anger freely on each other. The callous things they said to one another, their failure to listen, and the way they interrupted and "talked over" each other, as well as their body language demonstrating disdain and disrespect—all shouted out that I was in for a marriage counselor's worst nightmare. Yet, I had just been

through a similar horror myself in trying to understand and be understood in my former church. I knew
firsthand the reality of such frustration.

What I found bizarre about this first meeting was
that Don and Diane launched into their unrestrained,
pitched verbal battle the minute they entered my
office and kept up this combative clash for the entire
session, completely ignoring me. In addition, at the
end of the session, they walked out smiling! Before
they left, I was able to ask if they would like to return,
and they both beamed and said they would not miss
it, thanking me for doing such a wonderful job!

I was completely baffled, wondering what part
I had played in their pleasure. At the next session, I
found out. By then, they were ready to talk to me. Both
expressed their relief at finally getting to a safe place
(as I sought out the hospital in my own distress), in
the presence of trusted and caring persons, to safely
let their feelings out and off some steam.

I agreed that the previous session was certainly
steamy and asked how the week had gone after that
first visit. Don said he had hoped they would keep
talking, but it never happened. Diane agreed that they
did not dare talk for fear of repeating their performance in my office.

Both declared how frustrated and grieved they
were at their seeming inability to talk without arguing
and admitted that in fact at home they hardly ever
talked at all. Both complained how tired they were
of their dilemma. They felt imprisoned, even held in
bondage by a spirit of ill will. Both yearned for more

closeness and especially for ways of communicating better.

We all three agreed that any serious talking would be reserved for our sessions together. I praised them both for their honesty and wisdom in deciding to postpone the hard work of learning to communicate for their trips to my office. The motto was: "Small talk at home, big talk in the office."

The next week their statements of undying love and loyalty to each other further amazed me. I should not have been surprised, for I knew from long experience that people who care for each other can get very angry at each other. Don and Diane were not enemies after all, simply checkmated and stalemated. They really wanted to be helpmates, playmates, and soulmates and were frustrated, even depressed, by destructive habits, when what they really longed for was the pure and promising ideal of a mutually respectful, supportive relationship.

Just as I was still mourning the loss of a dream of my own, so they were both mourning the loss of theirs. They had a good dream, a worthy vision, abounding in hope of love and closeness. How well I knew that most deep disappointments occur in life when we long for and fail to realize cherished promises and possibilities.

I was thankful for the second session with Don and Diane, the session that brought out their admission of frustrated and hampered love—the real basis for their pain and suffering. Convinced they truly loved one another, now I knew how to proceed. From that point on, we would work together toward helping make their dream come true. All they needed was a little help, a few tools, and some new skills. They were open and eager to fit themselves into the role of students again.

Thank God, this lively couple was ready to work hard and finally learn to play. Now they are closer than ever to being helpmates, playmates and soul mates. God is indeed merciful, creating a miracle out of what I thought was going to be my most difficult couple. Don and Diane chose a scripture for their talisman, placing it on the refrigerator at home and on the dashboard of the semi Don drives over the road.

"Faith, hope, love abide, these three; but the greatest of these is love. Pursue love."
(1 Corinthians 13:12-14, 14:1)

Gratitude

Being a part of this couple's recovery from their grief was God's gift to me and reinforced what I had learned a year earlier in Arizona. As I had said in the previous chapter about the birds and the coyotes, with Don and Diane, I had the same sense of being invited, accepted and included in this lovely garden. They had thought they were coming to me for help, when in fact it was a mutual ministry.

Now I was being welcomed into my real garden, toiling and tilling to make health grow in the small confines of my office. Here was my real paradise found, and I was meeting this hospitality from strangers in need – I, a foreigner in their lives, who might become a healing friend.

The gratitude and joy I felt may seem unusual for a trained marriage therapist of many years experience. Yet, this success in my first month of resuming clinical practice was a boost to my confidence. When I first interviewed with the professional search committee of my new employers, I was nervous and somewhat apologetic about my recent hospitalization. After the interview, I was certain I had not measured up. To my delight and surprise, I was told I not only had the job but was hired because I had experienced hospitalization. Most of the board members were former clients of my gracious colleagues and were looking for counselors who had also known the path of healing first hand.

With that sort of support and understanding, I know that the work done in the next fifteen years would be one stimulated by gratitude and love. I think I can speak for Ruth as well as myself when I say our dream has come true. Our false dream is over. Today without a major rejection or loss, I can repeat my river wisdom with integrity and joy. The words came to me before I was ready to put them into practice in my life, not in the small church in the valley, but now so abundantly alive in the desert. As I had discovered by the Hassayampa's side, it is possible and life-giving to appreciate differences without having to differ, distinctiveness without disapproval, contrast without contrariness, being equal without being equivalent, being dissimilar without dissimulation, and standing alone without being aloof or lonely.

Such severe disapprovals, contrariness and dissimulations have been absent from my life for over a decade now, and I am far from lonely. However, I refuse to remain in naiveté and denial. I know that grief; pain and suffering are part of life, yet I hope never to be so rudely surprised again. My constant prayer is that I may be ready for whatever comes, expecting the best but open to the worst.

We are all in the safe arms of our Lord, and if we have them, families and friends. I have had the same experience in El Paso that I had arriving at the banks of the Hassayampa: "I came to this place troubled and in turmoil, and peace and refreshment came to me and comes to me much more often now. Something sacred and deeply moving has stirred me." – and continues to stir me still.

Questions to ponder:

1. Do you have a frustration you cannot solve? What is it, and what impartial person might you talk to about a solution? Is it urgent or important? How much or little will you settle for? Does scripture; especially the words of Jesus have any relevance?

2. Are you grieving any losses? Any major change is felt as a loss to some extent. What scripture passage helps the most in soothing your pain? Try Romans 8.

3. Is there someone in your life whom is difficult to communicate with? Who is the person, and is she or he aware of the hang-up? Might he or she be willing to work on it with you using these communication tools? Try listening for information only, without reaction or retort.

4. Open and honest communication becomes impossible when someone in the relationship misuses alcohol or other drugs. If this is a basic communication block in your relationship, how might you become willing to seek help? Try AA and Al-non. Seriously.

5. For one week, keep a little card handy to make a check mark for every I-statement and every you-statement you make, and then jot down ideas about how you can adjust the balance.

CHAPTER NINE

From Surprise to Surrender

—ⅢⅢ—

W ithout a doubt my favorite funny animal story came from a dear friend, Rod Haff, a member of the parish I served in San Antonio, Texas. Rod is a teller of tales, jokes, and anecdotes and a lovely human being. We used to have a men's organization known as the Men's Meat-Burning and Beverage Society, which met monthly at various homes for a cookout, refreshments, fellowship, and the latest jokes. Rod told this story almost every time we met. It was so good, and he told it so well with a Cockney accent, that it became a ritual that delighted us all. We laughed as hard the last time we heard it as we had the first time. To the best of my memory, it goes like this, with much more dialect understood:

"During the Second World War, as each new boatload of British troops Disembarked and assembled dockside after arriving in India, a sergeant major greeted them, who addressed them with this stern lecture on the dangers of jungle snakes:

'Gent'men, welcome to Injah. Whilst you're 'ere, you will encounter two kinds of snaikes. One is universally benign and the other is universally fatal. By far the most deadly serpent is the Yellow-Banded Krait, spellt, K-R-A-I-T. You will find 'em 'angin out o' trees. They are extremely easy to spot from the alternating 'orizontal bands of yellow 'n' black, yellow 'n' black, yellow 'n' black on their bodies, which are about two hinches wide and three to four feet long. "Now, if you run into one of these kraits, you better NOT run away else you're a goner. It'll catch you for sure and you will die in your tracks. You 'ave only one chance. You must attack. Sneak forward, grasp the snaike around the middle of its body with both 'ands and repeatedly and forcefully smash its 'ead against the tree trunk! That'll do the trick. Any questions? None, eh? Carry on.'

"A few days later the sergeant major was summoned to the hospital tent to visit a wounded trooper. He saw his soldier in traction, covered with bandages from head to foot. "What 'appened to ya, lad?" he asked.

"Well, it was like this, Sergeant Major. I was walkin' down this jungle trail and just like you warned, there was this yellow-banded krait, hangin' out of a tree, and I knew I was a goner if I ran. I froze and made sure. There it was – yellow 'n' black, yellow 'n' black, yellow 'n' black — just like you sez. So I sneaked up on 'im as careful as I could, grabbed 'im, and was about to bash 'is 'ead on the tree trunk, when I seen I was standin' there 'anging onto the tail of the biggest Bengal tiger in all Injah!'"

Crises and Surprises

Many of us know the saying —"having a tiger by the tail." A major factor in the success of the story is the element of surprise. The same thing happens in life. We encounter traumas in life that turn out far worse than we could have expected. Comedians thrive on the premise that things are never so bad, they could not be worse. Many of the jokes we laugh at fit this scenario of bad to worse. I believe we laugh in order not to cry. Fortunately, I have survived the times I thought I was bashing a yellow-banded krait, only to find myself hanging onto a ferocious tiger of a problem that came as an even greater surprise. It is a great relief to survive such shocks – cancer, depression, accidents, betrayals, rejections, false accusations, broken bodies, and a broken heart.

Going through one crisis after another with my father and all the sudden surprises with which he confronted me and mother, and how we managed to survive taught me to live with crisis and even thrive on it. My father needed money one time and sold all my possessions, including my bedroom furniture! He soon was in the hospital and I was without a bed. Mother and I calmly cashed in my savings bonds and bought another maple bedroom suite at Haverty's in Atlanta that my eldest daughter still has.

After leaving the hospital, my father sold my car. I was in college so I gladly did without the responsibility of car ownership. In fact, I was already so used to dad's scavenging any property of mine or mother's to keep him in booze that I never expected to hold on to much. I learned to roll with the punches. The difference in the degree of loss I felt had to do with how important the loss was. I could lose furniture, sporting equipment, jewelry, cars, clothing, keepsakes and any inanimate thing without much grief at all. All would be well, I thought. It would work out somehow. This sort of acceptance and optimism spread to more than lost things.

Blessings from Curses

In college my dream of being a world-class swimmer died as I left the swim team after my second year, yet, this gave me the time and opportunities to fall in love with learning, the Yale Library, trips to New York City with all its art and culture.

I fell into the ice covered Paradise Pond at Smith college while showing off my canoe skills. I developed bronchitis, which became asthma. This apparent disaster kept me out of the draft and duty in Korea, where many of my ROTC class were killed.

When I traveled to Europe, my suitcase was stolen yet found by the cab driver who noticed my Yale sticker on a suitcase carried by his fare to her apartment in Salzburg. He took me to the guilty woman front door, who burst into tears when she saw the driver and me confronting her. She begged to forgive her and stay with her and her daughter as their guest. I took her up on the invitation and she assuaged her guilt as she made amends by feeding and housing me in comfort and style for three weeks.

The CIA offered me a job after graduation which I accepted but suddenly changed my mind and went to work with my classmate's father, who was president of Revere Copper and Brass. Two of my classmates went with the CIA. and spent twenty years in a Chinese prison.

My choice to work with Revere Copper and Brass seemed a dead end and a waste of eight years in sales and marketing when I went to seminary yet, I later found the experience as a salesman to be invaluable in the ministry. I never made management. To this day, when someone asks me to pray for rain, I reply, "I am in sales, not management." Learning to convince and sell has been a blessing in disguise.

So, with these and many other fortuitous outcomes I have come to expect success out of failure, trusting survival's further blessings. Survival is one of life's greatest blessings, a blessing that should never be taken for granted. The saying "Hang in there" may mean hanging on for dear life, even if we have to hang on to a tiger's tail. Not letting go of some problems — the quality we call persistence — may be the only thing that keeps the tiger's claws and teeth away. On the other hand, not grabbing hold of some things in the first place—the trait we call precaution—can save us from many mistakes. Above all, knowing when to let go and let God is often the highest wisdom of which we are capable.

Humor

Becoming able at some point to minimize the impact of our mistakes by a good laugh makes life much easier. God's gracious gift of humor has helped me let go and let God many times. As human animals, we make so many absurd mistakes that God surely must have had many a chuckle at our foibles. My mother taught me by example to laugh at adversity and affliction. It was her best survival technique and mine. Someone remarked that human beings are the only animals that laugh and should be laughed at. Laughing *with* someone is even better. Thank God, I have a wife and family that love to laugh along the way.

One of the many reasons I love my wife so much is her charming way of laughing at herself when she makes a mistake. I laugh right along with her, and we enjoy our mistakes together, most of the time. She accepts the reality that she *makes* mistakes, while rejecting the possibility that she might *be* a mistake.

She has always inspired me not to take myself too seriously, nor to beat myself up when I miss the ball. Missing the ball is something I do quite often, particularly with my tennis friends, Tracy Baker, Steve Pell, Bill Updike, Tommy Posey and Jerry Dixon, who seem to enjoy the spectacle that I make of myself. I hardly ever take credit for accidental winning shots and base most of my play on accidents and amazing grace. What a relief to be human and fallible and have fun doing it. Being human and fallible in my case comes quite easily on the tennis court, since my lack of skill is obvious to everyone.

I recall the true story of a few men in a boat who, encountering a polar bear on an Arctic ice floe, sought to appease the bear by tossing it pieces of their lunch, chocolate bars and other treats. This worked fine until the bear polished off all the snacks then climbed into their boat with them and started sizing them up for lunch. I never found out what happened to those guys.

I even remember a cowboy in Sweetwater, Texas, during the Rattlesnake Roundup, who tried to kiss a snake "on the lips." He did survive the costly kiss, but only after losing his tongue and lower lip.

My own childish foolishness resulted in a bitten finger when I was told not to put it in a parrot's cage. Why do we do such dumb things? All creatures, human and animal, must share this blundering habit. Curious cats, dogs, and almost all infant animals have a playful and adventurous way of getting into trouble by mistake.

I am convinced, however, that most of our adult blunders are honest mistakes based on erroneous information, or sometimes on "stinking thinking." Hurt feelings generally stem from hurt expectations. Expectations arise out of our thinking process, from what we believe to be true. When we expect too much, too little, or a result that is unrealistic, or if we hold delusional beliefs, we are bound to be disappointed. We may truly be surprised, while an impartial observer may conclude that we should have known better in light of the facts.

A Supreme Surprise: Cancer

For years, I thought I was a healthy person. My doctors had declared how healthy and strong I was "for my age." Then, very much to my surprise, I discovered that I had cancer. Health flew from my mind and thoughts of disease and debilitation and death flew in. The plain and simple fact that a biopsy had found a significant cancer in my body immediately affected my identity. My sense of self was instantaneously altered. I became, from that hour of discovery, different. I was no longer healthy. Who was I? I was no longer even myself, but a "cancer victim," and with help and grace, soon become a "cancer survivor." Whatever the outcome of this dread discovery, I thought I would never be the same. I was right, but I never dreamed what the difference would turn out to be.

Although I was more conscious of the disease within me than the health left in me, I was in one respect, dealing with a common definition of health – as the absence of disease. My focus became, "What do I do?" The flip side naturally became, "What do I stop doing?"

The answers were obvious. We would spring into action and handle this crisis like all the other crises. We immediately canceled our vacation. Any other personal concerns and commitments would be set aside without a second thought. I would concentrate only on the horrendous fact of the cancer inside my body and my response to it became one thought: Get rid of the cancer somehow, some way, somewhere and soon! Then, I supposed I would be able to get on with being "who I really am" – a healthy person. I would only consider myself healthy when the disease was absent. The many options before me felt bewildering. I had to choose between ten different treatment possibilities, each with its pros and cons. As I prayed and shared my dilemma, I became aware that all my energy was focused on one outcome: to annihilate the cancer as quickly as possible.

It was exactly one month from the time I knew the bad news of cancer until I arrived at the hospital. At first, I was convinced that I could manage this crisis on my terms. I would not be the compliant patient. I would take charge of my own destiny. I would choose my course of action. No doctor would lead me by the nose. After all, I had more than thirty years experience as a minister, hospital chaplain, and mental health professional. I had helped others; surely, I could help myself. My self-confidence was enormous.

The day following my diagnosis, I traveled to the West Coast to attend a conference on "Spirituality and Healing" sponsored by Harvard Medical School. This trip had been planned for months – hardly coincidental. What could I possibly need more than a huge dose of God's spirit and his healing love? Immediately upon registering at the conference, who should I run into but my dear friend, Keith Miller, my rescuer from the valley church. Then I met an old college classmate, Tom Greening, I had not seen in forty-five years.

At first I kept the cancer secret, but not for long. Not only did I need to get the cancer out, I also needed to get my feelings out. The next day, after a troubled sleep, I eagerly sought out my friends to listen to my plight. I asked for prayers. I asked for laying-on of hands and anointing.

What I received in response to my fear and confusion was beyond my hopes. I was privileged to hear some of the most stirring, gracious and loving prayers in my life. I heard from speakers some of the most exciting, and yet humbling testimonies to God's healing I had ever heard. Half of these witnesses were in the medical field and the other half in the religious arena. What a gift to receive the day after I uncovered the existence of cancer to my friends.

My proud, confident spirit received its first drenching and dilution. My bravado was beginning to be whittled away. Tears came to my eyes. I shared my anxiety with my friends of old and with new ones I found. I received a new baptism of new love. The discovery of how much I was loved by at least a few friends was like a miracle of new birth. More than any learning in my life, I could never again deny the staggering fact of how much love there is in the universe – not just for me but for everyone.

The concrete, personal and genuine love I first received from Keith was quickly followed by more at the conference. This new appreciation of being loved so much has become a fountain of gratitude within me. I realized well in advance of my surgery, that the real source of health is love and that supreme love comes from the supreme Lover, our Lord Jesus

Christ. I sincerely believe that each gift of love has the Savior's stamp of approval on it.

All the love-experiences I felt from family, friends and caring strangers, which could easily be discounted as coincidences, were so numerous, so powerful and so full of compassion, that I could not ignore them. For me, they were the realities God used to lead me closer and deeper in faith. This trip was just the beginning. The additional mega-doses of love dispensed to me so generously by my precious wife, daughters, grandkids, in-laws and dozens of friends, colleagues, counselees, and church companions were beyond my comprehension. The showering of love so filled my spirit, that I surrendered with complete abandon to God and became healthier than I have ever been, long before I made my decision.

My choice was surgery. It had the best track record. All the other treatments required long stretches of time, ranging from a year to many years, with frequent visits to doctors. Surgery, on the other hand, would only take a few hours, and I knew I could not be at peace with the thought that the cancer was growing, larger and more deadly each day. I wanted it over and done. Any delay was unacceptable to me.

I recalled that, in any encounter with illness, Jesus never delayed. He healed on the spot. He drove out the demons. To me, the cancer was not mine. It was demonic. I would not embrace it nor own it. It was an invasion that had only one purpose - death. I would wage war against this "demon" with all my strength, with as many allies as I could muster, and with the skills of the surgeon. After I had the surgery, I told myself, I would recapture my old healthy self again

I must confess that the confidence I now place in God came from concrete and inescapable facts, not my initial faith. St. Anselm said, "Believe in order to understand." God, in his wisdom, let me strive and strain to understand before I truly believed. In this backward way, faith found me, even though I was going about it in the reverse order of Anselm. I was led through actual events, including conflicting medical advice, puzzling ideas and unexpected coincidence to holiness and the Holy Spirit.

I refused the preoperative valium. My daughter, Sandy, prayed the most loving and encouraging prayer in my memory as she and Ruth hugged and kissed me. I was glad to have a clear head to receive such precious love. When I finally slid my body onto the gurney that took me into the operating room, I experienced a surrendered composure within that could only be God's gift of grace. I was flooded with as much of God's presence as I could dare to receive. I felt healing energy and benediction. I experienced the name above all names, Jesus.

My greatest surprise (which was serendipity) was that my spirit was healed before my body was surgically tended to. The spiritual gifts prior to the surgery were sufficient. Whatever happened to my body in the operating room no longer mattered. I was already experiencing real health. God led me to understand that health is not the absence of disease, but the presence of God. I did not take myself on the journey to healing. I was led even though I tried to take the lead in the beginning.

The surgery was an enormous success. The cancer, according to the surgeon, was all gone. He cheerfully proclaimed, "We got it all!" I was relieved and thankful. My wife and daughters wept tears of joy. My friends rejoiced with them. I was on my feet the day following the surgery and discharged from the hospital the next. I was home free.

A lucky break? A healthy and strong patient? A brilliant surgeon? Yes, to some extent, all could be true. Yet far more significant to me than good fortune, my robust health, or the peerless skill of the surgeon, was the immense reality of God. What had happened anyway? I knew God produced and prompted my healing but I was healed on the inside, regardless of how the surgery turned out. The most amazing outcome was that God gave me his gracious gift of inner spiritual health in spite of my self-centered efforts to control events. This was my surgery, I had thought. I can manage crisis. I was in charge again and would survive and thrive in spite of everything. I had done this sort of thing hundreds of times. How wrong I was!

God did not favor me because of my good-ness, obedience, faith, energy, will, determination or any aspect of my being or behavior. God acted so wonderfully in my crisis to make the outcome a blessing, because God is God. The reality was and is, as it has always been: *This is the Lord's doing; it is marvelous in our eyes.* (Psalm 118:23). The message that defined my entire experience came from St. Paul in 1Corinthians 15:10, *"It was not I, but the grace of God that is with me."*

If the doctor had told me, he had failed and I had only a few years left, or less, I had been the recipient of benediction where it counted – in my spirit not my aging body, which will soon naturally die in a few years anyway. My experience led me to God in such a wondrous way, that what happens to my body now is irrelevant and will disappear in time. Yet, *"my soul magnifies the Lord and rejoices in God my savior."* (Luke 1: 46) and will continue such praise forever. I began more concerned with the flesh and met my own everlasting spirit – the best blessing. This grace can be everyone's, I believe, with all my heart.

Being a "cancer victim" or a "cancer survivor" became irrelevant. My identity was no longer shaped by disease, but by God and his saving health. Even if the surgical outcome had been different, I would still be inwardly healthy in Christ. No further visitations of disease, ill fortune or death will ever be able to take away what God has given.

My scripture emblem for this knowledge became Romans 8: 38-39 *"Neither death, nor life, nor angels, nor rulers, nor things present, nor things to come, nor powers, nor height, nor depth, nor anything else in all creation, will be able to separate us from the love of God in Christ Jesus our Lord" who* taught me, as never before that health and salvation are one and the same gift of grace. I was reminded that a state of grace is a state of health as well as a state of salvation. In fact, I recalled that the word salvation comes from the Latin, salvus, which means both salvation and health. Our word for healing balm "salve" comes from the same root word. I knew God was the "salve of my soul," my savior and my healer.

I find it interesting that some doctors speak of "not saving" their patients when they do not improve. No doubt, the salvation of patients is crucial to most doctors. Part of God's plan of salvation has always been mediated by our Great Physician, Jesus Christ whose will is health, whose will is salvation - here and now, as well as there and then.

Reflection on this reality has led me to be able to see, and to say, that all persons depend on God in Christ, whether we know it or not. My cancer experience shows me, too that this conviction has been the underlying, if unrecognized principle guiding my ministry. Through all the years I have served Christ as a parish minister and as a pastoral counselor, I have been devoted to the same "saving health" even without my total conscious knowledge. God heals by and through his love in the midst of stumbling efforts and in spite of mistakes. God can heal us spiritually, even though what we human beings define as "physical healing" never takes place. That is how I have experienced it. I thank God I now have a salvation memory, burned into my spirit, one that I will never forget and that I surrender to each day.

Jesus spoke to his contemporaries – admonished them, really – about not being able to recall the past or read the signs all about them — in other words, notice obvious reality. *"Do you have eyes, and fail to see? Do you have ears, and fail to hear? And do you not remember*? (Mark 8:18-19) I pray I never stop seeing and hearing the obvious.

It is difficult for human nature to change, and most of us haven't changed much since Jesus" day. Even now in the 21st century, many of us fail to check things out and rush to judgment without much thinking at all. This error can lead merely to inconvenience or misunderstanding, or it can end in suffering, as in my case with the valley church, or even tragedy when our mistakes are as spectacular and devastating as blundering into a tiger.

Immediately after my cancer surgery and while I was still on the mend, I began a series of counseling sessions with a young couple who came to me for marriage therapy – Sam and Harriett. I found that I was soon to be involved in a case of "mistaken identity" reminiscent of the tale of the yellow-banded krait, where expectations and blind belief led to major pain and grief. Fantasy and wishful thinking played a major role in this example of hurt expectations. My recent experience in the hospital and my renewed sense of hope in my own life spilled over into this new couple.

Sam's Surprise

Sam, a 29-year-old soldier had been married for three years to Harriett, who was then 22. Our first session together – the three of us – was extremely hopeful, loving, reconciling and full of promise for the future.

Yet, after scheduling at least eight more sessions, Harriett apparently had a change of heart and mind. Why? Neither Sam nor I knew. Whatever her reason was, she refused to return and went away to a distant city, even threatening to divorce. However, she would never tell Sam where she was and made calls to him on her cell phone. Her decision was a stunner, and naturally Sam and I were shocked, disappointed, deflated. What had happened? Now, what next? Sam was beside himself. For several sessions, all he could do was cry. He called me often on the phone at home. Fatherless, he was turning to me for parental guidance and support.

At first, Sam was in limbo. It was he who would have to turn loose of the tiger's tail. Harriett could not do it for him. In fact, Harriett was no longer his problem, since he was powerless over her and could not even find her.

At first, I too was at a loss, wondering how I could help. Harriett was gone but Sam was ever-present. I could only minister to him. Then I remembered that I did have at least one thing to offer Sam in the immediacy of his disappointment. It was hope. Hope that we both yearned for. I hoped we could find it together as we prayed for God's comfort and strength. Our prayers did not answer the mystery of Harriett, who is to this day still "about to" file for divorce — whenever she gets around to it. Nevertheless, we did find hope in the future.

Although I never mentioned my surgery and revitalized hope, my positive attitude seemed to bolster and cheer Sam. He did find help and hope, even though his marriage problem remains unsolved. He too learned to surrender and accept. He began to find himself. He saw his own mistakes. He realized how blind he had been with Harriett, who was still living the role of the pampered child, transferring her dependency from her mother onto Sam. He discovered she had a boyfriend. He even remembered how she objected to his having some dental surgery, because she refused to nurse and feed him for a few days. Incredulous at how much he failed to see, he realized the truth of the old saying — "love is blind."

Now the truth has dawned, and a new day is dawning with it for Sam. Today he is taking a long look at himself, his history, and his future. He has decided to be himself and work, with God's help, to "be the best he can be," a slogan that has taken on new meaning for this military man. He vows never to make the same mistakes and is taking some personality and psychological tests along with more counseling – to learn from his all-too-human mistakes. He keeps the scripture that has become his strength and hope on his refrigerator door:

> *"Therefore, since we are justified by faith, we have peace with God through our Lord Jesus Christ. Through whom we have obtained access to this grace in which we stand, and we boast in our hope of sharing the glory of God. And not only that, we also boast in our sufferings, knowing that suffering produces endurance, and endurance produces character, and character produces hope, and*

*hope does not disappoint us, because God's
love has been poured into our hearts through
the Holy Spirit that has been given to us."*
(Romans 5:1-5)

Together Sam and I are working on the affirmation that God, not Harriett, is his hope. If she comes back into the marriage, it will be by her choice *and* his. He refuses to have the old marriage, and will only settle for a new and healthy one.

Questions to ponder:

1. Have I ever taken hold of a "snake" only to find it was a "tiger's tail"? What was the situation, and how did it turn out?
2. Have I ever feared I would have to fight a "tiger," to discover later that it was only a paper one? What was that situation, and how did it turn out?
3. At a time when I was terribly afraid, where did I find my help? God wanted that help for you.
4. In a situation where I feel cornered and uncomfortable, can I ask my God to help me find a solution?
5. Can I name one or more ways I have found that help me let go and let God?
6. Reflect on the surprises in your life, especially curses that turned out to be blessings.

CHAPTER TEN

From Loneliness to Love

—ᴥ—

When I first met my wife, I knew she was a beautiful blessing. I should have also known Ruth was a gift of healing from our first date. Curiously, the first place we chose to dine and dance was the famed Owl Room in Atlanta's Henry Grady Hotel, with every table adorned by a small, smiling owl. Even though I knew this was a charmed evening, I presumed at first that all the charms belonged to this beautiful girl from Reading, Pennsylvania. The significance of the happy friendly owls was lost on me at the time. Now I am certain that Ruth and I were destined to have our "love at first sight" evening with more than mere human romance in store.

Today I know I was in the process of being forgiven and restored for my owl killing ten years earlier. This first owl evening was the beginning of my greatest happiness. My true life began that night with Ruth Clauser. Nine months later, we were married and traveled west as I began a sales career with Revere Copper and Brass, Inc. Although she still finds it hard to believe, I have experienced most of my benedictions from her.

In those early days of romance and love, owls were beckoning me, without my conscious awareness, back into peace and pleasure, instead of letting me stay stuck in the guilt and dread associated with my childhood offenses. Not only were owls apparently connecting with me in a benign and forgiving way, I was coming to know a young woman of wisdom — the legendary attribute of the owl. Ruth's depth of understanding of life, along with her unselfish love, has given our children and me great joy. None of my daughters would deny that Ruth Parham is as wise as an owl. Her wisdom is innate and angelic in its nature. She intuitively knows the right thing. If I had listened to her natural gifts of discernment more often, I am sure I would be much wiser today.

When our eldest daughter, Susan, was one year old, my mother taught her a delightful game called Owl Eyes. Much like peek-a-boo, this is a game of joyful surprise. With foreheads touching and eyes closed, on the count of three, both participants open eyes wide and exclaim "Owl Eyes!" Squeals of delighted laughter follow. I, too, played this game with all my daughters and grandchildren when they were in the baby to toddler stages of their lives. Maybe I am a slow learner; for once again, the significance of this newly discovered joy with owls was lost on me for a long time.

Now I know that the burden of guilt from a twelve-year-old boy's wanton and destructive act, which had weighed upon me for a decade, was being healed, and forgiveness was being offered in place of retribution. Moreover, most important, all this began with the advent of my new companion and growing family.

During our first years of marriage, Ruth's human imperfections and my own numerous flaws could never dampen our love for each other. Whatever rough spots we encountered as our differing personalities adjusted were nothing compared to the devotion we had for each other from the beginning. Such problems never stopped the flow of love.

Ruth has consciously poured so much love, affection and grace into our marriage and family that no recipient of her gifts could ignore such blessings. Provider of a "haven of blessing and peace" in our shared lives, she has also taught me how to be a better man, husband, and father. Above all she has shown me the way to live into our wedding vows to "love, honor, and cherish" one another.

Havens of Blessing and Peace

These familiar words from our Episcopal wedding ceremony hold great attraction and appeal. Surely, every human being has a great yearning for such havens. We long to live in a context of blessing and peace. I know that I ached for such a setting in which to live, for in my own family of origin, I had known just the opposite: a home of cursing and combat.

Far from being just plain blessed being there, I was usually "blessed out"—and old Southern expression for being roundly scolded or told off. I was frequently condemned, put down and emotionally wounded. Rather than living in peace, I lived in a land of continual conflict, oppression and outright hostility. The absence of sufficient blessing, approval and appreciation in that household was a source of tremendous pain for me. Was I foolish to hope for peace, safety and comfort in my future family? Certainly not! Ruth came into my life to invite me into just such a haven.

The word "haven" is very close to the word "heaven." Of course, expecting that our homes can be perfect havens or heavens on earth may be unrealistic. I hardly expected perfection. I just craved a little progress in heaven's direction. I knew I could never submit to a hell on earth as my old home had been. Well, I was surprised by joy.

"We can get better instead of bitter." During my prep school and college days, I had already begun to recognize the wholesomeness of this motto and choice. Intuitively, I knew I was heading in the direction of "better" rather than "bitter," supported by the angelic people in my life and my own attitude of stubborn optimism and persistent willingness.

My greatest desire was to have a family of my own — a family of blessing waiting to be embraced. When I embraced Ruth, I was suddenly having and holding my greatest desire, as she in turn took me "to have and to hold for better or for worse." What trust! To this day, she still holds me in sweet affection as her "precious Philip." Our wedding vows to love, honor, and cherish" each other have been our constant watchwords in Christ.

Love

Love is the first fruit of the Spirit named by St. Paul in Galatians 5:22. Love is indeed a spiritual treasure, a gift given by God. Yet, many of us never quite get it. We may give and receive lots of love, but often without perceiving that it comes from God. So many books have been written about love that any more words about it may seem superfluous. Nevertheless, I have been noticing a few new things about love, especially about "Love Himself."

Christ Jesus is our role model for love. He was and is complete and perfect love. We can learn from his example. One of the most comforting things I see in Jesus and his love is the way that he listens. Such compassionate understanding and empathy, full of concern for the other, must be divine. This quality of paying attention saturates Ruth. In fact, she likes to think of herself as "the nice lady who listens." Her sensitivity to others is remarkable. It is this focused and concerned interest in others that I missed in my father, and the same quality is also missing in many other families.

Ruth is seldom so worried about her own issues to the extent that she ignores her family and her friends. I cannot recall her overlooking, discounting or minimizing anyone. She seldom forgets others. I have often prayed that God would also help me become more attentive in this way. "Is that the truth, Ruth?" I will often jokingly ask. But I know it is. There is no pretense in her. She hardly ever pretends. In fact, she dislikes fantasy and science fiction of any kind. Reality is her choice. She keeps my feet on the ground, not to the fire.

Another very special part of love is allowing ourselves to be loved. Jesus actually reached out for friends and companions and was able to embrace and absorb their love. When we think ourselves unworthy, receiving love and attention from another may seem hard or even impossible. It is such fun to love someone who truly likes it!

I believe that Christ proclaims to us that we do have value, we do need love, we do want love and we do deserve love. He also taught us, through his frustrations in day-to-day life with his followers, and above all, by his sacrifice on the cross, that loving is hard work. Doing the work of love is not just a feeling of affection, but a difficult, demanding choice

Nevertheless, I know that Jesus had fun. He went to weddings rejoicing and seeing to it that the fun continued. Once a child himself, he certainly knew of children's games, especially Pipe-and-Dance, as evidenced by his criticism of the men of his generation: *"They are like children sitting in the market place and calling to one another, 'We played the flute for you, and you did not dance; we wailed, and you did not weep."* (Luke 7:32.16

I know of no one who loves my jokes as much as my wife. "Philip, you are a funny man," she frequently tells me, laughing. How many wives still say that after decades of married life? One of my delights in life is being our family's good-humor man. Both Ruth and I love to dance. We have learned much about jubilant play from one another. We have practiced on each other, our children and our friends. In my opinion, it is Jesus, the Lord of the Dance who issued our family license to practice his lessons of fun-loving and loving fun.

Honor

Honor is something we do not hear enough about these days. What does it mean to honor someone? The espousal and marriage vows use this word many times. What is it to say "I honor you in the name of God"? Honor is defined as esteem, treating one with worth and value, respect, showing consideration, admiration, appreciation, as well as exalting and recognizing the best, highest and noblest in a person Wouldn't it be grand and glorious to see all that honoring going on in every family, every workplace, in every church?

It was a great disappointment and a painful surprise in my marriage counseling practice to see contrary and opposite dynamics at work in so many relationships. Among intimate partners and family members, I have seen enough dishonoring, discounting, disrespecting, inconsideration, and depreciation to last me the rest of this lifetime and several more besides.

Perhaps part of our good fortune was - we worked hard at marriage. It was difficult learning to live and love together. It did not come naturally. One of the reasons I entered into the profession of marriage and family counseling is we needed it ourselves. We had to work so hard at times to understand and befriend each other. We went to a wonderful counselor in our

early marriage. What we learned and put into practice helped us develop healthier habits and launched
a renewed partnership. We became more fun and
functional.

We determined to put God and our relationship
first, even before children, church, business, friends
or family. Other important priorities came close
behind. Yet, our marriage was always our prime
human prerogative with others standing in line. This
mutual decision in itself was miraculous.

Hard work alone could not explain our good will
toward each other. In my mind, it was primarily the
respect and honor Ruth and I have always had for
each other. Another crucial element to our relationship is that we both truly like each other. Neither
of us can stand alienation, and I in particular have
an urge to "make up" and reconcile, find nursing a
grudge impossible, and feel an urgency to forgive
and be forgiven.

Ever since I heard Alexander Pope's aphorism,
"To err is human, to forgive is divine," I believe
forgiveness is from God. Jesus taught us in the Lord's
Prayer to pray for forgiveness. My assumption is that
forgiving is not a human asset but divine grace we
must pray for.

The other wonderful woman in my life, my
mother, taught me the truth of divine forgiveness,
how to edify and lift others up, not tear anyone down.
She showed me how to honor another. She knew the
wonderful secret that you can never lose by giving.
Even if there is no tangible gift in return, you always
win. Giving itself is its own reward. Showing honor

to another is such a gift. I learned to forgive as she forgave my father, over and over again. When I asked how she could do that, she said, "O, Philip, I don't! God does it all through me!" This is a gift I have tried to pass on from Jesus, from my mother, to my wife and family.

Cherish

Cherish is such a lovely word, an even lovelier idea. To cherish is to treasure. In French the word *chéri* means "dear one." To cherish is to hold dear with affection and tenderness, to nurture with great care, to support and sustain whomever and whatever we love

Such devotion enhances the twin aspects of love and honor. Honoring and loving require respect and allowing the other to be accepted as is, without attempts to reform and remake the partner. Cherishing holds fast to love and honor within the soul yet does not cling, bind or restrict the other. To treasure is to let the prize shine on its own.

Most of us are only too aware of the direct opposites of being appreciated and cherished, such as abuse, mistreatment, contempt and condemnation. Most counselors have to deal daily with such poisons to self-esteem. It would be a rare person who always treasures others. In contrast to most animals, we human beings do abuse, depreciate, maltreat, scorn and condemn each other – sometimes not even knowing we are doing it.

Why do we act in such cruel ways when we are called to regard each other as precious? The problem of evil is a mystery to me. Whether we base our understanding on the biblical story of Adam and Eve attempting to be as gods, or blame some resident and initial evil represented by the serpent, we are still left with the question, "Why?"

If we try to explain "sin and evil" as consequences of poverty, racism, prejudice, bad genes, poor government or many social causes, we are still faced with "Why?" We can only wonder at the exceptions to all these reasons. Why have not poverty and prejudice always produced shabby results and intolerance in return? How do we account for all the saintly and loving souls who come out of dire circumstances?

All I know about such weighty matters is that when it comes to relationships, we fail whenever we think we can depend on our own resources and then become grandiose. The curse of grandiosity invariably suppresses the gift of cherishing. Grandiose comes from two words found in similar forms in Latin, Italian and Spanish: "Gran" and "Dios" or "great god."

When we insist on being right and adopt attitudes of perfectionism and superiority, we become potential and, in extreme cases, actual perpetrators of evil. Conceit and complacency creates injustice. When anyone lives on a self-assumed level of infallibility and pride in relation to others, an offender is born. Offenders develop habits of looking down and putting down from their high horses, all others as less than. Anyone who is thus looked down upon can become a victim, if he or she accepts the stance of victimhood. The superior one then often goes on to unjust and evil acts against such, to his or her mind, inferior and wrong little ones, thus justifying injustice.

However this all came about, I think this painful mistreatment of the least of us is the source of human evil and cruelty. The writer of the apocryphal book, Ecclesiaticus said it well in chapter 10:13-14, 18:

"The beginning of human pride is to forsake the Lord; the heart has withdrawn from its Maker. For the beginning of pride is sin, and the one who clings to it pours out abominations...Pride was not created for human beings, or violent anger for those born of women."

We would do well to remember that Jesus is on the side of all the least, last, lost and lonely. It is only with God's help that we are able to do otherwise – to love, honor, and cherish each other, in the same way that God loves, honors, and cherishes us. Self-righteous and prideful persons cannot build homes that are havens of blessing and peace. Such homes arise out of partners' cherishing of each other and of the children who live in those homes.

Rewards and Punishments

Living on the Mexican border, I am used to hearing the word *precios*, meaning pricey, costly, worth a great deal. That is a perfect translation for the word "precious." If we would consider our true worth in the eyes of Christ, the cross becomes pure miracle and an unexpected blessing.

Why would God pay such a price? Perhaps this was the only way we would pay attention and see how much we are loved. Perhaps God blessed the priceless Son's sacrifice and self-offering on the cross to forgive, restore and *"deliver us from evil."* Perhaps we are loved so much that in spite of our cruelty and evil, Christ went through indescribable pain and suffering to embrace us all and solve our mysterious problem of evil for us with divine love. Our lives are very pricey indeed.

When I was a seminary student, one of my theology professors maintained that there were two approaches to ethics and moral behavior. One was an ethical system based on value and the good, while the other was based on behavior and good acts.

A value-based ethic stems from the innate goodness within a person, who does what is good because of an internal and resident good heart. Being precedes doing. A good person does good things. When St. Augustine said "Love God and do as you please," he was supporting such a view. The assumption is that if the love of God dwells within, good acts will follow. The outside will match the inside.

A behavior-based ethic, on the other hand, concentrates on doing, with the external action taking priority over the heart and inner intention. Outward standards determine correct conduct, irrespective of any innate goodness. Proponents of such a system believe the heart of humankind is corrupt and cannot be trusted. The Mosaic Law, based on command-ments and obedience to clear rules as the way to live, is grounded in such an ethic. The outside will rule the inside.

In my family life and my marriage, I have been influenced and motivated more by being than by doing. For me, what is in the heart, mind and soul is more important than happenings, actions and correct behavior. Report cards, medals, certificates of merit, awards, degrees, and outward applause for outer conduct have never come close to exerting an equiv-alent influence in my life to the value and goodness of another person's being.

A system of rewards and punishments never held much appeal for me unless the outcomes were fitting and proper as well as agreeable to the offender. When I served as chaplain in a prep school, I found that the most effective penalties were those selected by the student offender rather than by an adult faculty member. Invariably the student chose a harder penance for herself than the faculty member would have chosen. Penitentiaries were originally for peni-tents and those embracing sincere penance, for those who wanted to work through sorrow for their sins. I wonder how many convicts serving time today are truly penitent. Maybe it is time for us to spend more money on schools than prisons, helping educate people away from crime.

In my own life, punishment would always back-fire. Why? Because both rewards and punishments were meted out by people on high. I wanted to reap my own rewards, pat myself on the back, and feel the pride of hard-won achievements and accomplishments rather than being forced to show gratitude or think in terms of luck that some authority figure had declared my worth.

The statement "The teacher gave me an A (or an F)" is a lie. We earn our grades. Our learning is ours. Education, like any personal endeavor, belongs to us. All our actions are our own business and responsibility. No matter what talent we have and what circumstances surround us, each person is responsible to choose, to persevere, and to make the most of any situation. When we give teachers or parents the sole credit or blame for what we learn, we give up and "cop out."

It is true that in the words of Martin Luther King, Jr., "We cannot expect people to pull themselves up from their bootstraps when they have no boots." Yet, we all have minds, wills, dreams, desires and longings for discovery at some time in our early lives. The more we can be given and take appropriate credit for our efforts, the more satisfying will be the results. Even in the midst of dilapidated housing projects rife with gunfire and drugs, it is still possible for a motivated, determined person to claim his or her own way.

This strong conviction in me must have come about because my father's code was so unfair and brutal. My reaction to his injustices actually worked to my own advantage, teaching me to trust my own understanding and take responsibility for myself. Unfortunately, this led me into "works righteousness" and self-centeredness. Yet in God's wisdom this was a road I needed to travel down in order to find Christ. During childhood and adolescence, however, in spite of my own immaturity and wrongheadedness, I knew I could be more just and fair than my father was.

In parenting I relied on the principle that "conduct creates its own consequences." The moment a course of conduct is chosen, that choice creates consequences, some predictable, some not. In dealing with my children I used to ask, "Who does this belong to?" or "Whose name tag is on this?" or "Whose fingerprints will we find when we look?"

I wanted my children to be empowered by their own accountability, to know that the counting and accounting of deeds belonged in their hands. The dictum "If you broke it, you fix it" ruled in our home. Making amends and restitution were always praised more than mere perfunctory apologies.

Apologies are necessary, of course. However, an apology only begins the process. As soon as our children could understand the concepts, facing up and doing the repair work became the main outcome of misconduct, without any additional punitive measures. Cleaning the slate and removing the guilt by making amends provided the opportunity for closure and cleansing. The motto "I am responsible," so often repeated in AA, became our family slogan as well.

As parents, Ruth and I discouraged blaming, excusing, and trying to escape even accidental mistakes, for we believed that these tactics were disempowering, unhealthy, and shabby. Admission of deeds done was the honorable way, the honest admission ticket into recovery and redemption.

Accuracy, integrity and fairness were honored above all. Honesty always won.

Furthermore, we taught our children that breaking something, even a rule, is a thing, a happening, an occurrence, and a mistake that can generally be rectified. The actor is always more important than the act, the doer more important than the deed. I often tell my counseling clients, "You are never your diagnosis" and "You are always bigger and better than your problems."

To me, a person is precious without qualification. When working in hospitals, calling on the shut-ins, visiting the disabled and mentally impaired and even hearing the confessions of criminals, the one I try to see and value is the person for whom Christ died. These are the "little ones," the helpless and hopeless persons in dire need and circumstance whom Jesus called us to care for in spite of their inability to produce good works or show right behavior. Mother Teresa said she always tried to see such people as Christ in his most distressing disguises. All persons are precious, even pricey, no matter what. Without a doubt, Jesus focused primarily on the heart—on what is inside our spirits—and only secondarily on outward conduct.

Justice is mostly about conduct, good or bad, while mercy is mostly about our value and God's love for us. Many of us in Twelve-Step recovery programs have often said, "If I get justice for my life and past behavior, I have had it!" God may require justice, but I am grateful beyond words that mercy is loved even more. It was mercy, not justice that impelled Jesus to proclaim from the cross: "Father, forgive them for they know not what they do."

Every caring parent I have ever known has a love for his or her child that far outweighs hatred of that child's bad behavior. In addition, most good teachers lovingly remind their students that their grades are not a measure of their worth as persons but only a reflection of their performance at any given time. How fine it would be if every parent, every spouse, every boss and employer took the same approach. Good deeds are indeed important and necessary. Incompetence should not be rewarded yet shaming someone as "incompetent" and "inept" is cruel and unnecessary.

However angelic Ruth may seem to me and I to her, we both have behaved in unangelic ways. We are human, and at times, we have hurt each other. We occasionally disappoint each other. Even so, we know that to each other and in the eyes of God we are forever loved, valuable and worthy within. We shall always love each other for who we are, not for what we can or cannot do. When the day comes that because of sickness or old age we cannot do much at all, we will still be loved and be each other's beloved.

Once I thought that my mother and I were the only two persons in the world that mattered and we were prisoners in chains. Today, I am one of more than a dozen close yet unchained family members who miraculously like and love each other. I am sure this is God's doing and not my own.

Such graciousness and loving strength are far more important to my personal health and my integrity than I can ever express. Without my special angel of joy, my professional life in the ministry would have ended long ago. Were it not for Ruth's generous outpouring of love, would I now be celebrating my fortieth year in God's service? I can truthfully say that the last fifteen years have been the best years of my life. Perhaps the owls in my life have given me much more than their wisdom.

Two scriptures that have guided and inspired Ruth and me throughout our years together come from St. Paul's unfailing expressions of the joy he knows to be found in Christ, even in the midst of struggles and pain.

May the God of hope fill you with all joy and peace in believing, so that you may abound in hope by the power of the Holy Spirit." (Romans 15:13)

"May you be made strong with all the strength that comes from his glorious power, and may you be prepared to endure everything with patience and joy." (Colossians 1:11-12)

Questions to ponder:

1. Can you think of anyone who may have been an angel in your life? It might have been someone who had a word of encouragement when you were in despair, someone who offered a solution to a problem you had thought insoluble, or someone who came to you in spirit at a time of great need.

2. Have you known a home that was a haven of blessing and peace, and at some other time a home where there was cursing and combat? How does it make you feel to think about either one?

3. Is there something you can do to show another person that you truly love, honor, and cherish him or her?

4. Are you in or out of relationship with someone you wish would love, honor, and cherish you more? Can you think of some way to let that person know of your desire?

5. You may want to pray about one or more of the situations itemized here, asking God to help you see when angels have appeared in your life, what havens you have known.

CHAPTER ELEVEN

From Desire to Fulfillment

—⁓—

Picture this, if you will: a ragged and rumpled man, like so many homeless we have all seen too many times. He stands at the entrance of a magnificent cathedral, filled with worshippers. Summoning up his courage, this shabby person shuffles down the long center aisle, right up to the chancel steps leading to the sacred altar. Up he gingerly treads, shaking with obvious pain and what certainly must be - a lot of fear. With great difficulty, he limps forward and stops directly in front of two clergy who are offering Communion to the people, who are kneeling at the railing. One of the clergy holds a silver plate with bread and the other holds a cup with wine.

The raggedy man looks deeply into the twinkling eyes of the priest holding the bread, and asks, "Is that bread right there the body of our Lord Jesus Christ?" The priest responds, "I bet my life on it." With desperate and tear-filled eyes, he searches the friendly eyes of the priest holding the cup, "Is that wine in there, his blood?" "That is my belief," the priest gently replies.

"Well then, I sure would like to have me some of that!" he smiles. The celebrant responds, "I would be delighted. Have some." After cautiously taking a wafer and drinking a sip from the cup, both delivered with solemn words by each priest, the man straightens up, a look of peace radiates from his face; he turns on his heels and dances joyfully down the aisle and out the door.

Looking at him depart, the two priests turn to each other, place the holy elements on the altar, and with Olympic-winning smiles, shout "Yes!" as they "high-five" their hands in celebration. The cathedral grows silent as the echoes of their hand slap fade away. Then suddenly the entire congregation explodes with a thunderous, "YES!" and applauds as they turn to the exit where their rejuvenated brother had just departed. He had just been joyfully fed and refreshed with an ancient mystery of unspeakable healing peace that enveloped and blessed everyone.

Ever experienced anything like that? I hope you have. I am told it is a true story.

It almost goes without saying that a minister is immersed in so many blessed events full of joy and peace - births, baptisms, weddings, prayer and praise and preaching, home blessings, animal blessings, communion celebrations, sickbed anointings, confessions, absolutions, even burials. This God-incident should come as no surprise.

Yet for forty years, among my greatest joys, have been the private pain-filled moments in my study that somehow generated something extra special that led to joy-filled peace and celebration. Such shared joy out of shared pain has fed and watered my soul much more than merely feeling happy or experiencing ordinary pleasure. These are my cathedral moments - true moments of soul-arousal and spirit -resuscitation, when I am called upon to live out my calling - as a priest and as a fallible human being. Everyone can be a dispenser of grace to someone - someone yearning to have some of what you have to give - anyone.

My best moments in the cathedral, however, have been when not only giving but also receiving. Where have I found this - this give and take? In the fellowships of both Alcoholics Anonymous and Al-Anon. There I become the raggedy man and the raggedy priest. There I shuffle in pain up to an altar enveloped by the incense of caffeine and nicotine. Nevertheless, this special brand of "holy smoke" and constant coffee cups, can never hide the "twinkling and friendly eyes" of recovery, nor the source of the mercy I seek. There I find the "priceless gift of serenity" and more peace for my restless heart to rest in and more joy to dance to than any other place on earth. There I have learned that we are "not human beings <u>sometimes</u> living spiritual lives but spiritual beings <u>always</u> living human lives." For me this is fulfillment.

That is where I go in my desperation to plead, "I sure would like to have me some of that!" That program, that Big Book, those steps, those promises, those traditions, those slogans, those tapes and pamphlets - all grace, all blessing, all mercy. And I invariably receive the welcoming response, "We would be delighted, have some - and keep on coming back!" I never leave a meeting without at least one hug and without hearing some form of affirming applause - silent or audible.

If soul-sickness is the theme of our times, obviously soul healing and spiritual health are what we are seeking. My cathedral moments of healing and continued health have been with one foot in the church and the other in twelve-step recovery. Over fifteen years ago, I shared 365 of these dual moments in a meditation book called, *Letting God*. Let me share one such meditation (For Jan 28th) that for me embraces the essence of straddling both spiritual worlds, and echoes the AA slogan: "There but for the grace of God"

Jesus had told some scribes and Pharisees, who had caught a woman in the sin of adultery, *"Let him who is without sin among you be the first to cast a stone at her."* (John 8:7-11) No one could meet that requirement, so no stone was thrown. Justice was not served. She "got off." She was not innocent. Under the Law of Moses, she deserved her punishment - death by stoning. The Pharisees were right; she was wrong.

However, Jesus brought a new law into the world. This law is measured by mercy not justice. If we receive what we deserve, and if justice is served, no one is safe. We are all doomed. If we rely on justice, we've had it. Justice - When you get what you deserve. Mercy - When you do not get what you deserve. Grace - when you get what you do not deserve."

The Lord has all the help we need but do we believe it when we see it and when we hear it? The question is, "Do we want his help?" Jesus asked a blind man, "Do you want to see?" The blind man had been blind all his life, a beggar. That's all he knew. Jesus knew that such a man might not want unfamiliar sight. He also knew that health and the unknown challenges of a more responsible life could be fearful. It was a good question. With great courage, the blind man chose the path of sight.

I have often asked myself, "What do I want? Do I honestly want to take such a responsibility? Do I want to take admit my powerlessness, and that my life has become unmanageable? Do I want to believe that God can restore my sight? Do I want to turn my life and will over to God as I can and will know him in Jesus Christ?" Most of the time, I say, "Yes."

A funny thing about Jesus; he doesn't work against our will. He calls us, but he will not force himself on us. Yet he is always with us, maybe right behind us, just like our shadow. Until we turn and risk a look, he will not be present to us. The Son shines much better in our face, than in the shade behind our back.

Most of us have witnessed a three-year-old in the midst of a temper tantrum. Soothing and soft words fall on deaf ears. Shouting and screaming back at the child fail to work as well. Sometimes nothing seems to work. Often times such tantrums are cries for help, for someone else to take over. The fury is primarily from frustration with a situation too immense and overwhelming to cope with.

We also can behave like frightened and frustrated children. Life just often gets to be too much to handle! We cry out in exasperation and fury, "Please, please, for God's sake, somebody come and take this decision out of my hands, it's too big for me!" Then in the middle of our ranting and raving, in the midst of our thoroughly unacceptable behavior, we are picked up (still struggling and hollering) and put in our place. For a child that place is usually a safe place - a crib, a song, or comforting and strong arms. Just like a screaming child, we may be begging for someone or something to take away the frustration by taking over for us.

That is where the structure and strong arms of our Christian faith comes in - the safest place in the universe to be. When we "Let Go" of our need to be in charge and "Let God" take over, we can find the *"Peace of God that passes all understanding that will keep our hearts and minds in Christ Jesus."* (Phil 4:7) When we acknowledge god and pray "Thy will be done" and not "My will be done," then we can finally feel safe, secure and be at peace.

Albert Einstein once said: "The most beautiful experience we can have is the mysterious...Whoever can no longer wonder, no longer marvel, is as good as dead." If we begin to take a look at the mystery of the universe, we see that as our knowledge increases, so does the wonder.

Yet what about the mystery of faith? How to explain or comprehend the depth of our spiritual universe?

How can one human being in this vast universe be "Lord and God"? To even begin to answer that is like explaining the origin of the universe. The Incarnation of the Word made Flesh is as great a mystery. How do I relate to the vastness of our creation? How do I related to the enormity of Jesus the Christ, both God and Man? Our response to the world as well as our response to our Savior are both responses of faith: faith in the tangible and faith in the intangible. Thomas accepted only the tangible. Some of us also demand such concrete evidence. Yet, we have faith in astronomers' telescopes and findings as trustworthy without seeing or understanding for ourselves.

We also possess telescopes and findings - Holy Scripture. "Let Go and Let God" is more than just a slogan. It is the major theme of Christianity. Its findings are worthy of trust. Why not trust evidence whether it comes from the five tangible senses or the sixth spiritual sense - whether from science or spirituality? I naturally had to find this out the hard way. I wonder if there is any other way to learn. It is strange that I seem to remember what my tough teachers taught more than the easy ones.

The Call of the Owl

Forty years ago, a call to serve God and humanity snared me and has kept me a willing captive all these years. This call from God seems to have paralleled an owlish summons as well. From the moment of my "owl killing" at age twelve until today, I have become more awake and aware of a benign call from owls in my life. Growing beyond the fear and guilt of being a life-killer, I have heard the call of blessing and become devoted to helping restore life.

Owls represent blessings to me now, a symbol of all the grace and goodness derived from animals. If I were to craft a new coat of arms for myself, I would choose an owl as my ensign, for to me it stands for wisdom, an invitation to redeemed life and the mystery and sanctity of life.

Just recently, I happened to be looking at our old worn address book, containing years of names and addresses. On the cover was an illustration of a wide-eyed and smiling owl. How could I have missed this so often? Why an owl? Apparently, the illustrator thought an addressbook was full of people, the "who" list of the owner. Apparently, "who" and "hoo" are the mark and call of the owl, and fit the contents of the book.

There are certain owls that appear almost human to me. The snow owl and the barn owl both have flattened faces, wide eyes and small beaks that looks like noses. Eagles, hawks and other raptors could hardly be mistaken for people. For whatever reason, owls have become special, holy and significant to me. Like any symbol, the meaning is in the beholder, and there is no doubt that the *owl and I* are linked.

I am more aware than ever that I have been involved in this call and interest in the "who" questions and answers in the ministry and in counseling. Less important are questions of *what, when, where, why, and how* – which follow after the questions of being and personal integrity. The focus of any counseling is the person. Although I cannot claim an owlish wisdom, I can claim the curiosity of that call "Who are you?" People interest me as much today as ever before and animals are a new and exciting wonder to me as well. If the owl is my sign, then my song is "Getting to know you, getting to know all about you" from *South Pacific*.

The question of "who" is vast. Who is God? Who am I? Who are we? Who are you? Above all whose are we? God's. Who else would we want to belong to?

Our names, cultures, species, races and all other designations of all being, sensate as well as insensate, are our answers to "who" and "what." However, I have always been more interested in the personal aspects of life contained in "who" than the impersonal structures of "what."

The way we ask our "who" questions matters also. A guilt-ridden person may ask, "who am I? An "owl killer?" An aggressive and challenging way to ask is "who the _____ do you think you are?" A sympathetic and courteous way is "I am really interested in getting to know who you are." The astounded observer may ask, "Just who is that masked man?" A confused and suffering victim may ask, "Who am I, really?" The grandiose offender, in denial, may ask, "Who, me?" We all encounter these "who" questions everyday. As a counselor, I usually encountered the last two. These personal questions make up most our religious quests. We seek a personal encounter and yearn for a personal God. In the Bible the question, "Who are you?" is everywhere. The word "who" appears more than 3,000 times. Here are a few.

But Pharaoh said, "Who is the Lord that I should heed his voice and let Israel go? I do not know the Lord, and I will not let Israel go." Exodus 5:2

But to the one who had told him this, Jesus replied, "Who is my mother, and who are my brothers?" Matthew 12:48

Now when Jesus came into the district of Caesarea Philippi, he asked his disciples, "Who do the people say that the Son of man is?" Matthew 16:13

As a Christian pastor, I believe deeply in the "who" of life and in a personal Lord and Savior. It is he who has blessed me all the days of my life through pain and pleasure, depression and delight, fear and faith, anger and peace, loneliness and intimacy, guilt and forgiveness, shame and healing, sadness and joy. This experience has always been in relationships and among persons and personalities – human, animal and angelic. Because of this gratitude and positive attitude, this book has been filled with assertions of value, worth, hope, love, faith, courage, encouragement, cheer, compassion, along with acceptance of life as hard, confusing, unfair, tragic, painful, destructive and devastating.

The stories I have shared are about some very special "whos" in my life. The persons in these stories, including me, represent real life. Like life anywhere, it is the way it is – a mixed bag. Yet, this mixture of good and bad has always been God's "chili con carne, which "spices up" life and joy in spite of all the mysterious and emotional ingredients we put in our chili. I am blessed to have served a few bowlfuls to you.

Summary

—⁓—

Throughout this mixture of stories the saying "who you see is who you get" claims much attention. Who we see in ourselves and in others is vital to our view of life itself. In each story there is the tension between the "who" and the "what," between "being and doing."

Who a person is, one's identity, selfhood and authentic life all make up the essence of spiritual direction, though spiritual direction is not the same as therapy. Yet in therapy questions of being, worth, and existence are also the core questions. The reflective, contemplative, meditative, and inner conversations provide the major subject of such inquiries.

The person is a subject not an object. The *subjective* is full of "who" questions and interests, whereas the *objective* is more interested in "what and how" queries and concerns. Although both are important, I am convinced it is vital to first ask the question "Who am I" and "Whose am I" before I address the questions "What am I?" and "What do I do?" Over and over again, I have seen the "who" twisted and confused with the "what." Too many times the person is de-personalized. Too often, the person becomes a thing, a number, a consumer, an instrument to manipulate, a means to an end.

The first chapter, "From Anger to Courage" deals with anger as a personal protest against perceived injustice and self protection in Roger's story. God can redeem anger into strong courage and resolution, creating caring spiritual strength out of a difficult protective emotion.

My second chapter, "From Fear to Wisdom" tells how Bill's breakout from the fearful cage of his life as a victim began when he claimed his true self and came to believe in *who* he is, instead of seeing himself as the entity his women made him. We both discover the image of God to be not only being like God, but mostly being like God wants us to be and become.

With the third chapter, "From Pain to Sensitivity "my owl killing is revealed, where my actions – "what" I did – influenced my "who" conclusion – that I was a guilty killer. The blessings of pain and accountability are presented. God provides all the deliverance any one life could imagine.

The fourth chapter, "From Shame to Spirituality " recounts how Carol's controlling ways changed when she discovered her real spiritual identity as one who was imperfect and in need of letting go and letting God, rather than attempting to take God's place.

In the fifth chapter, "From Abuse to Friendship" I shared how believing in one's own conceit and importance and defining the self as one "who is in the center" keeps the self away from spiritual progress and away from the friendship, comfort and cure of being loved by Christ.

The sixth chapter, "From Vulnerability to Respect" introduces the tools of healthy boundaries and self-protection from being a "who" defined and shaped by others. Christ provides our sun and shield and teaches us self-respect and other-respect in the all for whom he died.

In the seventh chapter, "From Selfishness to Serenity," I share my own struggle with loneliness, who I was, am and will be. Claiming authenticity and integrity as my true self in need of love and relationships was a life-changing experience in which I found myself as a forgiven and healed person.

In the eighth chapter, "From Grief to Gratitude," loss, grief and depression are discussed within my life as well with Don and Diane, as they discover who they really are as a loving couple and claim their true marital identity. God's consolation and healing come in the midst of the valley of shadow and frustration.

The ninth chapter, "From Surprise to Surrender" shares my surprise visit by cancer and Sam's victimization and surprise are solved by self-acceptance, loving friends and God's grace.

In the tenth chapter, "From Loneliness to Love" I give thanks for "who I am" as the grateful life-partner of an angelic woman, my wife. She has helped me find my true "who" better than any human or animal in my life, as we both have found God's grace together.

My life and that of so many courageous counselees, family and friends has been one of continual uncertainty leading to faith, embracing hope and looking forward in love himself, Jesus Christ. The great Danish existentialist, Soren Kierkegaard's words capture my experience: "Life can only be understood backwards; but must be lived forward."

One last story truly reflects the wonder of "whoness": The only survivor of a shipwreck washed up on a small, uninhabited island. He prayed feverishly for God to rescue him, and every day he scanned the horizon for help, but none appeared. Exhausted, he managed to build a little hut out of driftwood to protect him from the elements and to store his few possessions. But then one day, after scavenging for food, he arrived home to find his little hut in flames, with the smoke rolling up to the sky. The worst had happened; everything was lost. He was stung with grief and anger. "God, how could you do this to me!" he cried. Early the next day, however, he was awakened by the sound of a ship that was approaching the island. It had come to rescue him. "How did you know I was here?" asked the weary man of his rescuers. "We saw your smoke signal," they replied. It is my prayer that some of my smoke came your way.

CPSIA information can be obtained
at www.ICGtesting.com
Printed in the USA
LVHW031244020221
678115LV00017B/357